13137

FLYING THE MAIL

TIME
LIFE ®
BOOKS

Other Publications:
PLANET EARTH
COLLECTOR'S LIBRARY OF THE CIVIL WAR
LIBRARY OF HEALTH
CLASSICS OF THE OLD WEST
THE GOOD COOK
THE SEAFARERS
THE ENCYCLOPEDIA OF COLLECTIBLES
THE GREAT CITIES
WORLD WAR II
HOME REPAIR AND IMPROVEMENT
THE WORLD'S WILD PLACES
THE TIME-LIFE LIBRARY OF BOATING
HUMAN BEHAVIOR
THE ART OF SEWING
THE OLD WEST
THE EMERGENCE OF MAN
THE AMERICAN WILDERNESS
THE TIME-LIFE ENCYCLOPEDIA OF GARDENING
LIFE LIBRARY OF PHOTOGRAPHY
THIS FABULOUS CENTURY
FOODS OF THE WORLD
TIME-LIFE LIBRARY OF AMERICA
TIME-LIFE LIBRARY OF ART
GREAT AGES OF MAN
LIFE SCIENCE LIBRARY
THE LIFE HISTORY OF THE UNITED STATES
TIME READING PROGRAM
LIFE NATURE LIBRARY
LIFE WORLD LIBRARY

FAMILY LIBRARY:
HOW THINGS WORK IN YOUR HOME
THE TIME-LIFE BOOK OF THE FAMILY CAR
THE TIME-LIFE FAMILY LEGAL GUIDE
THE TIME-LIFE BOOK OF FAMILY FINANCE

This volume is one of a series that traces the adventure and science of aviation, from the earliest manned balloon ascension through the era of jet flight.

FLYING THE MAIL

by Donald Dale Jackson

AND THE EDITORS OF TIME-LIFE BOOKS

TIME-LIFE BOOKS, ALEXANDRIA, VIRGINIA

Time-Life Books Inc.
is a wholly owned subsidiary of

TIME INCORPORATED

FOUNDER: Henry R. Luce 1898-1967

Editor-in-Chief: Henry Anatole Grunwald
President: J. Richard Munro
Chairman of the Board: Ralph P. Davidson
Executive Vice President: Clifford J. Grum
Chairman, Executive Committee: James R. Shepley
Editorial Director: Ralph Graves
Group Vice President, Books: Joan D. Manley
Vice Chairman: Arthur Temple

TIME-LIFE BOOKS INC.

MANAGING EDITOR: Jerry Korn
Text Director: George Constable
Board of Editors: Dale M. Brown, George G. Daniels,
Thomas H. Flaherty Jr., Martin Mann, Philip W. Payne,
John Paul Porter, Gerry Schremp, Gerald Simons,
Nakanori Tashiro, Kit van Tulleken
Planning Director: Edward Brash
Art Director: Tom Suzuki
  Assistant: Arnold C. Holeywell
Director of Administration: David L. Harrison
Director of Operations: Gennaro C. Esposito
Director of Research: Carolyn L. Sackett
  Assistant: Phyllis K. Wise
Director of Photography: Dolores Allen Littles

President: Carl G. Jaeger
Executive Vice Presidents: John Steven Maxwell,
David J. Walsh
Vice Presidents: George Artandi, Stephen L. Bair,
Peter G. Barnes, Nicholas Benton, John L. Canova,
Beatrice T. Dobie, Carol Flaumenhaft, James L. Mercer,
Herbert Sorkin, Paul R. Stewart

THE EPIC OF FLIGHT

EDITOR: Dale M. Brown
Senior Editor: Jim Hicks
Designer: Raymond Ripper
Chief Researcher: W. Mark Hamilton

Editorial Staff for *Flying the Mail*
Picture Editor: Robin Richman
Text Editor: Russell B. Adams Jr.
Writers: Robert A. Doyle, Adrienne George, Laura Longley,
Glenn Martin McNatt
Researchers: Carol Enquist Beall, Dominick A. Pisano
(principals), Marguerite Johnson, Elizabeth L. Parker
Assistant Designer: Van W. Carney
Copy Coordinators: Elizabeth Graham, Anthony K. Pordes
Picture Coordinator: Betsy Donahue
Editorial Assistant: Caroline A. Boubin

Special Contributor: Nancy Cromwell Scott (research)

Editorial Operations
Production Director: Feliciano Madrid
  Assistants: Peter A. Inchauteguiz, Karen A. Meyerson
Copy Processing: Gordon E. Buck
Quality Control Director: Robert L. Young
  Assistant: James J. Cox
  Associates: Daniel J. McSweeney, Michael G. Wight
Art Coordinator: Anne B. Landry
Copy Room Director: Susan B. Galloway
  Assistants: Celia Beattie, Ricki Tarlow

Correspondents: Elisabeth Kraemer (Bonn); Margot
Hapgood, Dorothy Bacon (London); Susan Jonas, Lucy T.
Voulgaris (New York); Maria Vincenza Aloisi, Josephine du
Brusle (Paris); Ann Natanson (Rome). Valuable assistance
was also provided by: Helga Kohl (Bonn); Lesley Coleman,
Jeremy Lawrence (London); Cheryl Crooks (Los Angeles);
Donna Lucey (New York); Mimi Murphy (Rome); Janet Zich
(San Francisco); Akio Fujii, Kazuo Ohyauchi, Katsuko
Yamazaki (Tokyo); Traudl Lessing (Vienna).

THE AUTHOR

Donald Dale Jackson, a former staff writer for *Life,* has written two volumes for Time-Life Books in the American Wilderness series: *Sagebrush Country* and, with Peter Wood, *The Sierra Madre.* He spent a year at Harvard University as a Nieman Fellow. Among his other books are *Judges,* a history of the United States judicial system, and *Gold Dust,* a narrative history of the California gold rush. For *Flying the Mail,* he traveled extensively, interviewing individuals associated with the airmail's early days.

THE CONSULTANTS for *Flying the Mail*

Jesse Davidson, an avid collector of photographs of the United States Air Mail Service and chronicler of its past, is the owner of the extensive Jesse Davidson Air Mail History Archives in New York City. A licensed pilot and retired editor of aviation magazines, he began his research into the airmail in the early 1950s, gathering materials from early ground personnel and pilots. He is the author of *Famous Firsts in Aviation.*

Roger E. Bilstein, Professor of History at the University of Houston at Clear Lake City, Texas, has extensively researched the early United States airmail and its socioeconomic impact. Also a specialist in aerospace, he was a Visiting Scholar at the National Air and Space Museum in 1977-1978. He received the Goddard Essay Award of the National Space Club in 1978 as well as the Manuscript Award of the American Institute of Aeronautics and Astronautics in 1979.

THE CONSULTANTS for *The Epic of Flight*

Charles Harvard Gibbs-Smith was Research Fellow at the Science Museum, London, and a Keeper-Emeritus of the Victoria and Albert Museum, London. He wrote or edited some 20 books and numerous articles on aeronautical history. In 1978 he was the first Lindbergh Professor of Aerospace History at the National Air and Space Museum, Smithsonian Institution, Washington.

8963

Dr. Hidemasa Kimura, honorary professor at Nippon University, Tokyo, is the author of numerous books on the history of aviation and is a widely known authority on aeronautical engineering and aircraft design. One plane that he designed established a world distance record in 1938.

For information about any Time-Life book, please write:
Reader Information
Time-Life Books
541 North Fairbanks Court
Chicago, Illinois 60611

©1982 Time-Life Books Inc. All rights reserved.
No part of this book may be reproduced in any form or by
any electronic or mechanical means, including information
storage and retrieval devices or systems, without prior written
permission from the publisher, except that brief passages may
be quoted for reviews.
First printing.
Printed in U.S.A.
Published simultaneously in Canada.
School and library distribution by Silver Burdett
Company, Morristown, New Jersey.

TIME-LIFE is a trademark of Time Incorporated U.S.A.

Library of Congress Cataloguing in Publication Data
Jackson, Donald Dale, 1935-
  Flying the mail.
  (Epic of flight)
  Bibliography: p.
  Includes index.
  1. Airmail service, United States—History 2. Airmail
service—History. I. Title II. Series.
HE6496.J3   383.144'09   82-2020
ISBN 0-8094-3329-X   AACR2
ISBN 0-8094-3330-3 (lib. bdg.)
ISBN 0-8094-3331-1 (mail order ed.)
ISBN 0-8094-3332-X (deluxe ed.)

CONTENTS

The daring young men of the "suicide club"

When Dean Smith, an Army flying instructor during World War I, decided to join the U.S. Post Office Department's fledgling Air Mail Service in 1920, his fellow pilots at New York's American Flying Club thought he was crazy. In those days the airmail, Smith later explained, was "considered pretty much a suicide club"—and for good reason. Established in 1918 with a handful of adventurous young aviators and a few fragile Army trainers, the service prided itself on flying the mail in all kinds of weather, in spite of accidents that claimed the life of one pilot in six in 1920 alone.

Airmen who were willing to risk such grim odds were a rare and intrepid breed. Discovering that their planes' few instruments usually failed to function, they became masters of aerial improvisation. To compensate for compasses that frequently strayed a full 90 degrees from the proper heading, pilots flew low enough to follow the trustworthy "iron compass"—railroad tracks. When fog, rain or snow threatened to blot out their view of known landmarks, they resorted to time-tested formulas like this one: "After you cross the railroad tracks pull up into the soup, count to thirty, then let down—that way you'll miss the high tension lines."

In the decade that followed World War I, airmail pilots practiced seat-of-the-pants flying at its best, with many a forced landing and many a long trek to the nearest farmhouse. Sometimes the fliers' hairbreadth escapes were bizarre, and occasionally they were amusing enough to joke about, like the crash landing described by Smith in this telegram: ON TRIP 4 WESTBOUND. FLYING LOW. ENGINE QUIT. ONLY PLACE TO LAND ON COW. KILLED COW. WRECKED PLANE. SCARED ME. SMITH.

Membership in the "suicide club" demanded supreme courage and endurance, but to pilots who survived its trials, flying the mail was a career like no other. "Alone in an open cockpit, there is nothing and everything to see," wrote Smith. "It was so alive and rich a life that any other conceivable choice seemed dull, prosaic and humdrum."

E. HAMILTON LEE

A flying instructor for the U.S. Army during World War I,
E. Hamilton Lee pioneered the airmail routes between Chicago
and St. Louis and Minneapolis and Chicago. By the time he
retired, in 1949, he had logged more than 4,000,000 miles.

SECOND LIEUTENANT JAMES C. EDGERTON
Lieutenant Edgerton—shown accepting a congratulatory
bouquet from his sister—flew from Philadelphia to Washington
on May 15, 1918, the first day of regular airmail service. He later
became the Post Office's chief of flying operations.

MAX MILLER
*Born in Norway, Miller left home to become a sailor
at the age of 14 but soon abandoned that calling for aviation.
The first civilian pilot to be hired by the United States Air Mail
Service, Miller proved invaluable as a scout for new routes.*

RANDOLPH G. PAGE
On September 8, 1920, Page flew the New York-to-
Chicago leg of the first transcontinental mail flight. A colorful
character, he was said to have consumed two quarts
of whiskey once while flying between Omaha and Chicago.

WILLIAM "WILD BILL" HOPSON
Hopson once entertained the citizens of
Bellefonte, Pennsylvania, a stopover on the mail run, by
bicycling down the steps of their courthouse. He died in 1928
when his plane crashed in bad weather en route to Cleveland.

JAMES H. KNIGHT

Knight became a national hero in February 1921 when he
flew through the night from North Platte to Chicago to
save the first continuous coast-to-coast mail flight from failure.
He had broken his nose the week before during a crash landing.

CARL BEN EIELSON
The first pilot to fly the mail in Alaska, Eielson charted the
route between Fairbanks and McGrath in 1924. Renowned
for exploratory flights in the Arctic, he perished in 1929 while
flying to rescue the passengers of an icebound ship.

HAROLD T. "SLIM" LEWIS
*Slim Lewis flew the Omaha-to-Cheyenne leg of the airmail's
first regularly scheduled night flight on July 1, 1924. "He was
the ace of the whole bunch," remarked a field clerk. "He
always got through, it seemed, when others couldn't."*

London postal workers load a 23 ½-pound bag of George V coronation mail, Britain's first official airmail, into a Blériot monoplane for the 20-mile flight to

1

A new venture in the skies

As the crowd at London's Hendon Aerodrome pressed around Gustav Hamel's 27-foot-long Blériot monoplane, the young English pilot glanced warily at the leaden clouds that scudded overhead. He was eager to get off the ground, but on this ceremonial occasion, the inauguration of a special airmail service commemorating the coronation of King George V, there were formalities to be observed. Hamel shook hands with the assembled well-wishers, graciously accepted a silver medallion bearing the image of a small airplane and listened to the inevitable speech praising him and his fellow fliers for their services to "this new science of aviation."

Finally, Hamel climbed into his Blériot, revved up his 50-horsepower engine and thundered down the runway as the crowd sang "God Save the King" and soldiers sent the Union Jack racing up a flagpole. It was 4:58 on the afternoon of September 9, 1911, and the first officially organized airmail flight in the British Isles was under way. In the 23½-pound mailbag attached to the plane were commemorative letters destined for the German Kaiser and the Emperor of Japan, and a militant manifesto from British suffragettes to Prime Minister H. H. Asquith: "Remember!" it said, "votes for women in 1912." Among the many messages to the new King was one signed by the three pilots who would be flying this 20-mile airmail route between London and Windsor Castle. The aviators congratulated the sovereign for having this pioneering service launched during the first year of his reign and concluded prophetically: "We believe this important event will become Historical, and its development will lead to a revolution in the present modes of conveying communications between the peoples of the world."

Fifteen minutes after takeoff, Hamel touched down on a meadow not far from Windsor and yielded his mail to the local postmaster for delivery. Over the next two weeks, Hamel and the two other coronation mail pilots logged 19 more flights between London and Windsor, and the special cards and letters that they carried became instant collectors' items. Public reaction to the flights was generally favorable, though a dubious Manchester *Guardian* intoned that the experiment "demonstrated nothing except the ardour with which grown-up people will throw themselves into a game of make-believe."

It was a game that would turn into serious business within a few more years. And then, for nearly two decades after their tentative first flights, aerial couriers would be in the vanguard of civil aviation, leading the

Windsor on the 9th of September, 1911.

A bicycle postman hands over coronation airmail to the mustachioed mayor of Windsor. Pilot Gustav Hamel, bareheaded at center, flew beyond the planned landing site, and the postman had to cycle to the plane to accept the delivery.

way for the great commercial airlines that would one day span whole continents and oceans. Often flying at night with only the most rudimentary navigational aids to guide them, these bold airmen with their cargoes of letters, packages and postcards would pioneer the air routes over formidable mountain ranges and sprawling deserts. Among them were many whose names would be all but forgotten, and others who were destined for immortality. One was the romantic Frenchman Antoine de Saint-Exupéry, a key figure in France's spectacular drive to carry airmail down the forbidding west coast of Africa and across the South Atlantic to Latin America. Another was Charles A. Lindbergh, perhaps the greatest pilot of them all. They differed in their capacities, and in their ultimate renown, but they had in common their daring and a singular dedication to flying the mail.

The notion of carrying mail in airplanes had been flickering in the imagination of the aerial-minded almost as long as the idea of powered flight. As far back as 1843 a prescient Briton named William Samuel Henson had applied for a patent for a "locomotive apparatus" intended to transport "letters, goods and passengers from place to place through the air." In 1910, nearly seven years after the success of the Wright brothers at Kitty Hawk, Claude Grahame-White in England and Glenn Curtiss in the United States had flown unofficial airmail flights. But in the same year, the United States Congress rejected the first legislative proposal for an experimental airmail route.

At an agricultural and industrial exhibition in Allahabad, India, Henri Pequet stands by the propeller of his Sommer biplane before making the world's first official airmail flight on February 18, 1911. The Frenchman flew some 6,500 letters five miles in 13 minutes.

Inspired by Britain's coronation mail flights, a cocky Achille Dal Mistro grasps the wheel of his Deperdussin monoplane, ready to take off with Italy's first trial airmail on September 19, 1911. The flight from Bologna to Venice took 88 minutes.

Governmental faintheartedness could not persist indefinitely, however, and in February 1911 Britain became the first nation to sanction an airmail trial when a flight was staged at the United Provinces Industrial and Agricultural Exhibition in Allahabad, India. Pilot Henri Pequet, a Frenchman, hauled some 6,500 cards and letters over a five-mile route in a Sommer biplane that had been shipped to the site in a crate.

It may have been a curious coincidence that fliers from three other nations—France, Italy and the United States—went aloft on mail flights within two weeks of the initial coronation mail delivery, but it was more likely a sudden flowering of the nationalistic competition that aviation so often inspired. Whatever the reason, the French sent an aerial postman winging between Casablanca and Fez in French North Africa—a harbinger of the great international airmail network that France would one day create—only four days after Hamel's maiden postal voyage; the Italians followed six days later with a flight between Bologna and Venice. The Italian inaugural was apparently a consolation prize for pilot Achille Dal Mistro, who persuaded the Bologna postmaster to let him take off with the Venetian mail after his plane was delivered too late for a race he had planned to enter. Dal Mistro's glory was only slightly tarnished when his plane crash-landed, with no harm to either the pilot or the mail, on the Venice Lido.

Earle Ovington, a beetle-browed American who had learned to fly in France, got the United States mail airborne on September 23 at an aviation meet at Garden City, Long Island. Seeking publicity for their show, the promoters had obtained government permission to fly cards and letters from the airfield, and a temporary post office branch was set up to handle the mail. During the nine-day event, Ovington piloted a cramped Blériot monoplane—named *Dragonfly* for the insect it resembled—on a series of six-mile round trips between Garden City and Mineola, where he dropped his mail pouch in a field for the postmaster to retrieve and consign to the regular postal system. The specially can-

celed mail so rudely delivered was primarily of interest to stamp collectors, but Postmaster General Frank Hitchcock—who came to observe the proceedings—was sufficiently impressed that he went up for a spin in a Curtiss biplane and came down with visions of a Congressional authorization of $50,000 to get regular airmail service under way.

The chief attraction of sending mail by air was speed, though doubters often pointed out that the fastest aircraft of the day (Ovington's Blériot had a top speed of 59 miles per hour) would probably lose a race with a train. And speed had an almost automatic fascination for Americans. As far back as 1834, a United States Postmaster General had decreed, in the roseate language of the time: "The celerity of the mail should always be equal to the most rapid transition of the traveler." In other words, if a train was faster than a horse, mail should be sent by train. But his 20th Century successors in the postal bureaucracy would spend years trying to convince skeptical bankers and businessmen—seen as prime users of the service—that airmail would save them time, and thus money, by speeding the transfer of funds and documents.

When the speed argument faltered, the proponents of airmail in America could fall back on the airplane's capacity to surmount natural

Leather-helmeted Earle Ovington accepts the first sack of official United States airmail from Postmaster General Frank Hitchcock at a Long Island aviation meet on September 23, 1911, as other postal officials look on. Ovington flew the mail six miles from Garden City to Mineola.

Ovington's Blériot, the Dragonfly, swoops over the temporary post office tent at Garden City's airfield. During his one-week stint, Ovington carried 43,247 pieces of mail, balancing the pouches on his lap because his cramped monoplane did not have the room to stow cargo.

barriers. Indeed, the Congressional proposals that surfaced with relentless regularity from 1912 on emphasized the advantages of airmail in such trackless country as Alaska and the desert West. But this argument ignored the limited carrying capacities and flying ranges of the flimsy aircraft of the time; a plane that could haul only the thinnest mail sack and travel no more than 100 miles or so on a tank of fuel would not be of much use in Alaska. Perhaps mindful of these shortcomings, congressmen repeatedly rejected the airmail bills presented to them.

For a time, while other nations made halting attempts to deliver mail by plane—Japan and Germany launched short-term efforts in 1912, and Italy was operating an irregular mail service by 1917—the American airmail service was little more than a sideshow. Post Office-sanctioned mail flights became standard features at numerous aviation meets held throughout the country. Clerks at a special postal substation at the air-show site would process cards and letters, and then a pilot would fly the mail sacks to the nearest post office for delivery. Meanwhile, the show would proceed with such popular events as a plane-mounted pigeon hunt or a three-man parachute drop.

By 1916, however, the American attitude toward aviation was chang-

A French Breguet tractor biplane the Arabs called "the flying tent" takes off from Casablanca in 1911.

Europe's leap into the future

In monoplanes and biplanes just a few years advanced from the Wright brothers' earliest craft, adventuresome European pilots eagerly took to the skies in the three years before World War I to fly the Old World's airmail.

Their primitive planes varied from the Morane-Saulnier in France *(right, center)* to the popular Farman III in England *(below)*. Among the fastest was the German Otto *(right, above)*, capable of a top speed of 69 mph.

Many of their flights, including some of the firsts pictured here, were more symbolic than practical. But in proving that mail *par avion* could speed communications, these planes and their pilots gave new meaning to the word "progress."

Built of mahogany and ash covered with cloth, a Farman III carries Britain's coronation mail in 1911.

An Otto biplane driven by a 100-hp Argus engine arrives in Munich in 1912 with Bavaria's first airmail.

A Morane-Saulnier with a 60-hp Gnôme engine awaits takeoff from a Parisian suburb in 1913.

A German Euler biplane named the Gelber Hund, or Yellow Dog, delivers mail to Darmstadt in 1912.

ing. War had broken out in Europe in 1914, and reports from the battlefronts left little doubt about the airplane's military value. This strengthened the hand of the airmail boosters in the Post Office Department and Congress, enabling them to overcome the stubborn fact that popular demand for regular mail deliveries by air was almost nonexistent; now it could be argued that mail flying would be excellent training for military pilots. The Post Office seized the moment to advertise for private bids on eight proposed mail routes, seven to Alaska and one in Massachusetts, but the single bid that came in was rejected because the bidder had not posted the required bond. Congress finally bestirred itself and authorized $50,000 for an experimental airmail service. The United States was now in position to launch what would eventually be one of the world's most ambitious and enduring airmail operations.

It was perhaps inevitable that such a system would be born in the sprawling United States rather than in the more geographically compact nations of Europe. Some 2,500 miles separated the population and financial centers of the East Coast from their counterparts on the West Coast, and Chicago was farther from San Francisco than London was from Moscow. Even the fastest trains took about four days to span the continent; if this time could be trimmed by airmail planes, then the two coasts and the great cities in between would be bound that much more closely together. America, with its penchants for speed, commerce and national unity, could hardly resist the notion of an aerial mail service.

The task of designing a feasible plan and assembling the necessary ingredients to bring such a service into being fell mainly to Second Assistant Postmaster General Otto Praeger, a scrappy and tenacious Texan who had learned his way around Washington as a newspaperman and later as the city's postmaster. Praeger found an important ally in the National Advisory Committee for Aeronautics, an independent government body with an interest in promoting aviation. He and the NACA agreed that their best chance for success was to abandon the idea of establishing mail routes in such difficult and distant precincts as Alaska and to concentrate instead on the shorter and more populous corridor between Washington and New York.

America's entry into World War I in April 1917 placed a new obstacle in Praeger's path: He was unable to acquire planes because the War Department needed all that American manufacturers could produce. Fortified with a fresh $100,000 Congressional allocation, however, the persistent Praeger and his friends at the NACA hammered away at the War Department with the argument that mail service would train Army pilots in cross-country flying. The impasse was finally broken in February 1918 when the War Department agreed to furnish both planes and pilots to fly an experimental route. The Post Office and the Army would operate the service jointly, with the Army providing mechanics and the Washington landing site; the Post Office would contribute the New York and Philadelphia fields, the clerical staff and the fuel.

The Post Office moved quickly and arranged for landing strips at New

York's Belmont Park—a race track on Long Island—and at Bustleton, in North Philadelphia. Praeger issued press releases trumpeting the advent of same-day delivery for letters mailed as late as noon between Washington and New York. Then the Army, suffering a last-minute attack of cold feet, tried to call the whole thing off two weeks before it was due to start. Praeger responded by asserting that the Post Office would carry on alone if necessary; the Army relented and detailed Major Reuben Fleet to take charge of the planes and pilots. Captain Benjamin Lipsner volunteered to handle administrative matters and to supervise the first day's flights out of Washington, scheduled for May 15.

"The free channels of the open air will formally be thrown open to the U.S. mail," *The Washington Post* exulted on the morning of the 15th. A more cautious if somewhat naïve note was sounded in a Post Office press release of that same date. "It is possible that there may be some days when fog will interfere with the landing," it said. "It is not anticipated that this will occur frequently, if at all."

Ben Lipsner was not quite so optimistic. He had spent most of the previous night roaming the deserted streets of the capital, thinking about the things that could go wrong. The plan called for Army pilots flying Curtiss JN-4H biplanes—an advanced version of the standard, single-engined Jennies that the military used to train cadets for service in France—to ascend from Belmont Park and the old Polo Grounds in Washington's Potomac Park. The planes would land at Philadelphia, where fresh planes and pilots would carry the mail the rest of the way. The 204-mile trip between New York and Washington was expected to take three hours.

During his sleepless night, Lipsner fretted that President Woodrow Wilson, who led the list of dignitaries invited to witness the Washington takeoff, might decide not to come, thus damaging the event's publicity value. Even worse, what if the President showed up and something awful happened? The plane that was to carry the mail from Washington was not even in the city yet; it was due to be flown in that morning from Philadelphia. What if it did not make it? A mechanical breakdown, for any of a dozen reasons, could force a cancellation and send a disappointed President back to his limousine. There was even the possibility that the plane could fail to clear the high trees that surrounded the small Polo Grounds field. The tormented Lipsner finally forced himself to eat a leisurely breakfast before walking past the Washington Monument and over to the field. Along the way he noted gratefully that the weather was clear and bright; that banished one anxiety.

Reaching the nearly deserted Polo Grounds more than two hours before the scheduled 11:30 takeoff, Lipsner found that the plane had not yet arrived. Rushed to completion only the day before at the Curtiss plant on Long Island, the craft was being ferried from Philadelphia by Major Fleet, who had taken off at 8:40 after suffering through a night as long as Lipsner's—spent making last-minute repairs on the Jenny and its 150-horsepower Hispano-Suiza engine. The flier who had drawn the

honor of making the maiden postal voyage out of Washington, Second Lieutenant George L. Boyle, had not yet arrived either. Boyle, who had only recently received his wings, had been selected less for his flying skill than for his political connections; his fiancée was the daughter of Judge Charles McChord, an Interstate Commerce Commissioner who had won the gratitude of postal authorities by opposing a takeover of the parcel-post service by private express companies.

Early-bird spectators, drawn by the publicity surrounding the flight, had already begun trickling in before 9:30. The still-jittery Lipsner, glancing up from an inspection tour of the turf that would serve as a runway, noted desolately that no one from official Washington was among them. Then at 10:35 Fleet's Jenny glided over the trees and swerved past the bandstand at the far end of the field. The onlookers rushed forward as Fleet rolled the plane to a stop and got out, but policemen kept them in check.

With Fleet's arrival the field seemed suddenly alive with activity. The leather-jacketed Boyle had finally appeared, and now, his aviator's goggles pushed up on his forehead, he stepped forward to study the

President Woodrow Wilson congratulates Major Reuben Fleet, in charge of the Air Mail Service's Army planes and pilots, on the initiation of airmail between Washington and New York on May 15, 1918. Among the guests at the Polo Grounds is the Japanese Postmaster General, on Fleet's right.

map—an ordinary road map—that Fleet spread out on the side of the plane. Mechanics rushed up with tools and bent over the engine.

The eminent guests so nervously awaited by Lipsner began to arrive: the inventor Alexander Graham Bell, Arctic explorer Admiral Robert Peary, Postmaster General Albert S. Burleson, Senator Morris Sheppard of Texas, a longtime airmail champion, Navy Secretary Josephus Daniels and his assistant, 36-year-old Franklin Delano Roosevelt. The crowd, estimated by a *Washington Post* reporter at several thousand, buzzed with excitement. Finally a caravan of automobiles drove up and President and Mrs. Wilson emerged, accompanied by Secret Service men and more reporters. The President's hand was bandaged as a result of a burn he had suffered when he had inadvertently touched a hot exhaust pipe at a recent Army tank demonstration. His wife carried a bouquet of flowers for pilot Boyle.

A moment later a Post Office truck pulled up alongside the plane and workers transferred the 140-pound mail pouch from the truck to the forward cockpit of the Jenny. Boyle climbed into the rear seat and strapped himself in. A mechanic standing by the propeller shouted, "Contact," and Boyle turned on the ignition switch. The mechanic pulled hard on the prop, but the engine coughed once and died. After three more tries the engine still would not catch. Then Lipsner heard a voice behind him say: "We're losing a lot of valuable time here." It was the President. Lipsner's midnight dread seemed about to be realized.

Fleet, who had flown the plane only an hour earlier, ordered his chief mechanic to check the spark plugs—nothing wrong there—and then the fuel tank. It was nearly empty; no one had remembered to refill it after Fleet landed, and with the plane in its tail-down, parked position no fuel was reaching the engine. No one had thought to have a supply of gasoline on hand, either, so the red-faced mechanics quickly drained fuel from other planes parked nearby and filled the tank. They cranked the prop again, and the engine responded with a gratifying roar.

President Wilson and the other relieved onlookers watched Boyle taxi into position and then take off over the trees, clearing them by what looked to Lipsner like three feet. But as the craft climbed and then turned, Lipsner had the uneasy feeling that something was not right: The pilot seemed to be heading in the opposite direction from Philadelphia. The melancholy confirmation came about an hour later when Lipsner received a telephone call from a chastened Boyle; he had flown south instead of north, he reported, because his compass "got a little mixed up." He had landed on a plowed field near Waldorf, Maryland, 25 miles from the capital, and broken his propeller in the process. A truck was dispatched to pick up the mail.

Fortunately for the future of airborne mail, the other three opening-day flights turned out to be less eventful than Boyle's. The dignitaries invited to the New York ceremonies saw First Lieutenant Torrey Webb consult his watch, board his plane and take off with minimal fanfare in the middle of an oration by the president of the Aero Club of America.

Webb touched down an hour later in Philadelphia, to the immense satisfaction of another large crowd of spectators, some of whom clutched red-white-and-blue cards announcing the airmail timetable.

A scant six minutes after Webb landed, Second Lieutenant James Edgerton was airborne with the Washington-bound mail. His plane appeared over the Washington field at 2:50, only 20 minutes late. The pilot's little sister rushed forward to give him a bunch of roses.

The last aerial postman to go aloft that day was First Lieutenant H. Paul Culver, who drew the Philadelphia-New York leg. Anxiously scanning the sky for the overdue Boyle, Culver waited nearly an hour past his scheduled departure time before getting orders to take off anyway, bearing only the skimpy Philadelphia-to-New York postal payload. When he appeared over Belmont Park at about 3:30 he was joined by an escort of seven planes from the nearby military field in Mineola. According to *The New York Times,* the craft were "darting and diving like birds at play," but Culver's first words after he landed were anything but elevated: "Where can I get a quick lunch quickest?" he asked.

The journalistic coverage of the airmail's debut dispelled any apprehensions that Lipsner might have felt about the public's reaction to the event. Boyle's embarrassing waywardness was barely mentioned in the rush of congratulatory comments. The respected aviation journal *Aerial Age Weekly* called the first day's runs a "great success" and noted that postal officials were already talking about adding airmail routes to Boston, Pittsburgh and Cleveland; *The New York Herald* proclaimed that nothing "short of a hurricane" could stay these brave new couriers, while the *Scientific American* reporter, whose vantage was the New York field, was charmed by the "total absence of that incessant tinkering which we generally connect with air flights."

The giddy reverie of the morning-after reviews made it easy to overlook the formidable obstacles that lay in wait for an enterprise this adventurous—barriers that ranged from zero-visibility weather to unreliable machines and from mountainous terrain to the minefields of politics. The trouble started on the second day, when Second Lieutenant Stephen Bonsal, the son of a well-known war correspondent, lost his way in fog over New Jersey and came down on the horse-filled infield of a race track in Bridgeton. Swerving to miss the thoroughbreds, Bonsal slammed into a fence and damaged his plane. Then on the following day, George Boyle proved once again that he lacked the keen sense of direction required for cross-country flying.

Reuben Fleet, asked by the Post Office to give the well-connected Boyle a second chance at the Washington-Philadelphia run, decided that this time he would escort the young pilot as far as the Baltimore area to see that he was on the right course. After Fleet turned back to Washington, Boyle's instructions were to keep the Chesapeake Bay on his right, a flight plan so faithfully followed that Boyle wound up several hours later at Cape Charles, Virginia, having flown a nearly 360-degree course around the bay. Taking off again after refueling, he managed to reach a polo field near Philadelphia before he ran out of fuel and crash-landed, breaking a wing. Fleet rejected a Post Office request that Boyle be given yet a third chance, and sent him back to flight school.

Given the inexperience of Boyle and his comrades, the frequently difficult weather and the absence of any reliable navigational instruments, the biggest surprise attending the United States Air Mail's beginnings was not that it sometimes failed but that it succeeded as often as it did, all without fatalities or serious injuries. The Post Office, displaying an affection for airmail statistics that it would retain through nine adventurous years, reported after two weeks of operations that 53 out of 60 flights had reached their destinations without unscheduled interruptions. Two weeks later, it was announced that three of the four first-day fliers—Edgerton, Culver and Webb—had soared through a month of operations without mishap.

Even so, there were signs of trouble ahead. One was the chronically light loads the planes were carrying; on many days the pilots could have tucked their postal cargo into their jacket pockets. This struck a particularly sensitive nerve at the Post Office, which was determined to justify the service on economic grounds. The airmail pilots' first encounters with severe storms signaled another potentially troublesome development: a damn-the-weather-the-mail-must-go-through mentality. Lieutenant James Edgerton, who survived one flight on which at 10,000 feet "everything vanished in a turmoil of storm, rain, hail and lightning," believed that in so doing he had conquered "the psychological dread of bad weather"—and that other pilots could do the same. Edgerton's conclusion was important not only because it coincided with Otto Praeger's own opinion that weather should be no barrier to mail flights but also because Edgerton was soon to become chief of flying operations. *Aerial Age Weekly,* the airmail's most consistently enthusiastic advocate, echoed the same theme when it commented that "the pilot must take a chance and fly under almost any conditions" except those conclusively deemed impossible.

The Post Office's demands for dependable daily (except Sunday) service regardless of weather clashed with the Army's reluctance to risk its planes and men for the mail while there was still a war on. By July the uneasy partners had agreed to terminate their joint venture in August, when the Post Office would receive a shipment of six new planes from the Standard Aircraft Corporation of New Jersey. The planes, though equipped with the same 150-horsepower engines as the Jennies, were faster and could travel farther on a tank of fuel.

The new aircraft had been selected by Ben Lipsner, who had, at Otto Praeger's persistent request, resigned his Army commission to become superintendent of the new Air Mail Service. Lipsner's next job was to recruit a corps of civilian pilots to fly the mail. The chief prerequisite, a minimum of 1,000 flying hours, effectively limited the candidates to men who had served as Army instructors. The first to hire on was Max

Nattily attired Harry Mingle, president of Standard Aircraft Corporation, presents Second Assistant Postmaster General Otto Praeger with delivery papers for six new mail biplanes at the company's New Jersey plant on August 6, 1918.

Miller, a fearless pilot who would soon court and marry Lipsner's stenographer. The addition of three other fliers—former automobile racer Edward V. Gardner, ex-barnstormer Robert F. Shank and veteran test pilot Maurice A. Newton—completed the nucleus of what would eventually become a remarkably gifted and courageous company of airmen.

On August 6, Lipsner, Praeger and other Post Office officials traveled to Elizabeth, New Jersey, for a round of speechmaking and the formal delivery of the new Standard planes. Lipsner spoke of the "atmosphere of romance and wonder" that still surrounded aviation but added that the Air Mail Service had shown that planes could be practical commercial vehicles as well. "We pass," he said, "from poetry to mathematics." Then pilot Eddie Gardner took one of the new mailplanes aloft and flew a series of acrobatic maneuvers for the crowd, promising afterward that he would eschew stunting while on duty.

With the Army out of the picture, the Post Office could no longer claim that the Air Mail Service was of any value in training military pilots. But airmail supporters in both the government and the press saw no reason to cut back. On the contrary, they wanted to expand. The most persistent and articulate of the boosters was an Italian expatriate and aviation writer who had been born Mario Terenzio Enrico Casalegno but had anglicized his name in America to the less mellifluous Henry Woodhouse. A founder of the aeronautical journals *Flying* and *Aerial Age Weekly* and an officer of the prestigious Aero Club of America, Woodhouse had been plumping for airmail since long before it was fashionable or even sensible. He viewed the New York-to-Washington line as merely a short-term preliminary to a nationwide network of mail routes, which in his opinion should begin soon. In fact, he had already published maps of proposed air routes, including a coast-to-coast flyway that was astutely named the Woodrow Wilson Airway.

In Otto Praeger, Woodhouse saw the perfect instrument of his ambitious vision. Praeger, too, spoke incessantly of expansion in all directions, of night flights and multiengined mailplanes and even of routes beyond America's borders. And he was in a position to turn his ideas into action. In June he had approved a demonstration flight to Boston, and in August he announced plans to extend the service westward to Cleveland and Chicago.

Max Miller and Ed Gardner were selected to survey the proposed route in a two-plane test flight that would mark the new Air Mail Service's first encounter with the Allegheny Mountains—a challenging barrier not because of their elevation but because of the scarcity of level landing sites and the unpredictable and often foggy weather along the way. Miller and Gardner would also be testing the merits of two types of aircraft: Miller was to fly a Standard with a 150-horsepower Hispano-Suiza engine; Gardner, accompanied by mechanic Edward Radel, would pilot a Curtiss R-4 with a 400-horsepower Liberty engine.

When Lipsner briefed the two pilots on the flight, he was not above exploiting their natural rivalry. Their refueling stops, he explained, were

Lock Haven, Pennsylvania, Cleveland and Bryan, Ohio, 160 miles east of their goal of Chicago. Miller, flying alone, would take off first, said Lipsner, and Gardner, with his mechanic, would follow. "What do you mean, follow?" Gardner exploded. "Do you think I'm a baby?"

Lipsner then said that Gardner could leave first. "I couldn't follow him for a mile without running him down," Miller retorted. It would be, of course, a race, but Lipsner tried hard to convince his pilots that flying time and performance counted more than who got there first. Miller won the right to start first in a coin toss. When Lipsner had completed preparations for the flights, he left for Chicago—by train.

The weather in New York was dark and forbidding when Miller prepared to take off from Belmont Park on the morning of September 5. "Look me up when you get to Chicago, Max," Gardner shouted cheerily. "I'll wait for you," Miller replied. Miller lifted off at 7:08, climbing through a layer of clouds and leveling off at 5,000 feet, with another cloud bank above him. Two hours later he nosed through the mist and landed in a field near Danville, Pennsylvania, to find out where he was.

Airmail superintendent Benjamin Lipsner, second from left, shows off the first civilians hired to fly the post in August 1918. On the left is Edward Gardner; to the right of Lipsner are compass expert Maurice Newton (the only new airmail pilot over 40 years old), Max Miller and Robert Shank.

Gardner, meanwhile, broke a tail skid on his takeoff run and had to switch to another plane, finally getting away at 8:50.

Lipsner, waiting at the Chicago post office for his special telephone to ring, heard first from Miller. "Where's Eddie?" Miller asked. "Never mind Eddie. Where are you?" Lipsner replied. "Lock Haven," said Miller. "Radiator's leaking." Lipsner, noting that Miller was on schedule, told him to have the radiator fixed and get on his way.

Twenty minutes later the phone rang again. It was Gardner, who had fought his way through a storm only as far as Wilkes-Barre, 80 miles short of Lock Haven. "Where's Max?" he asked. Told that Miller was already at Lock Haven, Gardner climbed back into the storm but was soon forced to land again to get his bearings; airborne once more he had to land yet again, this time with engine trouble. It was 2:16 before he beat his way to Lock Haven.

Miller was already gone by then, but he was having troubles of his own. An overheated engine forced him down on a Pennsylvania pasture, but a suspicious, shotgun-toting farmer ordered him back into the air. Miller made two more brief stops to water his radiator and flew on to Cambridge, Ohio, where he was pleased to learn that Gardner was still in Lock Haven, grounded by weather and engine problems. Miller had to wait for another two hours in Cambridge while the radiator was patched up again; after two additional stops he finally put down at 8:25 p.m. on the outskirts of Cleveland. Lipsner, whose goal had been to have both pilots in Chicago by nightfall, took what solace he could from the fact that they were still intact.

Miller's irksome radiator kept him in Cleveland until 2:15 the next afternoon, by which time Gardner was nearing the city; he was at last making a race of it. Miller stopped for 30 minutes at Bryan, taking off at 4:55. Gardner landed at 5:01. Two hours later Miller's plane appeared

Max Miller's Philadelphia-bound Standard dusts cheering spectators as it takes off on the Air Mail Service's initial flight from College Park, Maryland, on August 12, 1918. On this inauguration day of the civilian-run airmail, College Park replaced the inadequate Polo Grounds as Washington's postal airfield.

over the landing field at Chicago's Grant Park, where a large crowd had turned out to greet the mailplanes. He landed to deafening cheers. Spotting Lipsner as he unbuckled his belt, he yelled: "Where's Eddie?" Lipsner told him that Gardner was close behind, but Miller, believing that his fellow pilot had taken a shortcut over Lake Michigan in an effort to catch up, fretted that he had lost his way in the darkness. He volunteered to take off again and look for him, but Lipsner said no. A few minutes later Gardner called from Westville, Indiana, where he had run out of daylight. He flew into Chicago the next morning.

A few days later, Gardner managed to salvage his share of glory. Lipsner, still anxious to prove that a mailplane could get from Chicago to New York between morning and nightfall, sent the two pilots back to New York a day apart. Miller suffered still more radiator problems and had to quit for the day at Lock Haven; Gardner, still flying with a mechanic, made it through to New York in a record 9 hours and 18 minutes flying time. Everything went well until the landing, when Gardner misjudged his altitude in the darkness and smacked down too hard on a field in Hicksville, Long Island, ripping off the landing gear as the plane somersaulted. But Gardner and his mechanic escaped with minor injuries.

Despite the grave weather and mechanical obstacles laid bare by the Miller and Gardner flights, Post Office officials saw the pathfinding mission as an unqualified success. The only route change that seemed necessary was a switch from Lock Haven to nearby Bellefonte, Pennsylvania, as the midway stop between New York and Cleveland; both pilots had complained about the mountainous approach to Lock Haven. The Postmaster General announced in October that regular ser-

Preoccupied with his map, Max Miller is greeted by Paul Brosius, the postmaster of Lock Haven, Pennsylvania, while his Standard's leaking radiator is filled by mechanic Albert Cryder on September 5, 1918. Miller's goal was to beat fellow pilot Ed Gardner on their pathfinding flights for the New York-Chicago mail route.

vice to Chicago would begin in December, as soon as the postal fleet could acquire more planes. Mail couriers would leave both ends of the 711-mile run at 6 a.m. throughout the winter. The time allowed for the trip, including stops at Bellefonte and Cleveland, was 10 hours.

In November, however, the picture changed dramatically. The War was over, and hundreds of military planes—among them the British-designed, American-built de Havilland 4s, equipped with powerful 400-horsepower Liberty engines—would be immediately available for civilian use. The Armistice would also liberate hundreds of trained pilots, many of whom would no doubt leap at a chance to shift from combat missions to mail flying. The possibilities seemed almost endless, and Praeger envisioned the rapid establishment of 50 new mail lines employing 1,000 pilots. The routes would crisscross the nation—New York to San Francisco via Chicago, Washington to San Diego via San Antonio, Norfolk to Los Angeles, Bangor to Key West. Testifying before a Congressional committee, Praeger provided an extra fillip: "But here is the big thing," he said. "In the spring we are going to fly at night." The mail would leave Chicago at 9:30 p.m., the Second Assistant Postmaster General explained, and arrive in New York the next morning.

But such bold plans would not be carried out by Ben Lipsner, who had objected from the start to Praeger's decision to launch Chicago-New York service in the dead of winter when flying conditions would be at their most hazardous. This was not his only disagreement with the headstrong Praeger. He also resented the increasing pressures to hire and promote men whose only qualification seemed to be their solid political connections. The final blow came in late November, when Lipsner returned from a business trip and found that Praeger had fired Eddie Gardner for prudently refusing to fly in a fog that cut his visibility to a mere 25 feet. On December 6, after trying unsuccessfully to reconcile his growing differences with Praeger, Lipsner turned in his resignation; Max Miller quit the next day, announcing that he had no confidence in an airmail service stripped of Lipsner's leadership.

While it was still reeling from the highly publicized departures of Miller and Lipsner, the service was struck by its first fatal accident. Carl Smith, a former Navy flier who had just joined the Post Office, was test-flying a D.H.4 on December 16 when the plane stalled at 200 feet and plunged to the ground. Smith was killed instantly; witnesses speculated that he might have survived if the pilot's seat had been in the rear cockpit, which had been converted to a mail compartment.

Two days later Praeger's grandiose master plan suffered an even more severe setback. Pilots and planes were deployed at various points between Chicago and New York for the official opening day of nine-hour service between the nation's two largest cities. Praeger, Woodhouse and other dignitaries gathered at Belmont Park at 6 a.m. to watch pilot Leon "Windy" Smith take off on the first lap, to Bellefonte.

Smith had been airborne only a few minutes when he returned to the field with engine trouble and switched to another plane. On his second

This Standard JR-1B, decorated with a mail pouch painted on its side, was piloted by Max Miller on the first civilian mail flight, from Washington to Philadelphia, in 1918.

A standard of excellence

The Standard was one of the most widely used planes of its day, despite an early setback that almost ended its career before it began. Designed in 1916 as a trainer for the U.S. Army, the early Standard was fitted with a four-cylinder Hall-Scott power plant that had a tendency to catch fire in mid-air; the Army grounded the plane in 1918 in favor of the structurally similar but more reliably engined Curtiss JN-4, or Jenny.

The Standard got a new lease on life just before World War I ended. Re-engined with a 150-hp Hispano-Suiza motor, the Standard displayed the superior aerodynamic qualities that led the Post Office to buy six for use as mail carriers. With a top speed of 100 mph and a range of 280 miles, the Standard was cheaper to operate than the Jenny and could fly more than twice as far on a tank of fuel.

try he lost his way and set down at State College, 11 miles southwest of Bellefonte. The pilot on the Bellefonte-Cleveland leg flew on without the mail from New York but could not find the Cleveland field and landed 10 miles away. A backup flier crash-landed and flipped his plane over at Painesville, Ohio. Two planes set out from Cleveland to Chicago; one hit a fence on landing at Defiance, Ohio, the other, piloted by Carroll C. "Mike" Eversole, limped into Chicago too late in the day to begin the return flight to Cleveland. Beleaguered but unbowed, Praeger sent his de Havillands up again on the 19th and once more on the 20th, but both times they were brought down by engine failures; most of the mishaps were caused by overheating.

Eager to prove the airmail's possibilities to an increasingly indifferent public and a dubious Congress, the postal barons had leaped before they looked. Pilots had been sent to fly hastily tested planes over a difficult and inadequately explored route with which they had little familiarity. Most important, the de Havillands were simply not fit for the demands of airmail duty, especially long-distance and low-altitude flying. Among their more serious shortcomings, as identified in the postmortems, were the location of the pilot's cockpit, weak fuselage frames and a flimsy landing gear with undersized wheels. The Post Office drew up new specifications and invited manufacturers to submit bids for the modifications. New York-to-Chicago service, not to mention the loftier dreams of night flights and transcontinental routes, would have to wait for better planes.

The nearly forgotten New York-to-Washington line was meanwhile operating briskly—though Praeger reported revenues of $60,653 and a net deficit of $8,969 for the first six months. And he was undaunted by the onset of winter. "The mail has been carried in blinding rain and hail, on fogbound days with visibility of not over half a mile, and in the face of gales," he boasted.

Pilots were frequently disquieted by such foul-weather flights but learned to take them almost in stride. E. Hamilton Lee, who joined the Air Mail Service in late December, was approaching Belmont Park from Philadelphia on a particularly murky day when he strayed too far out over the Atlantic and suddenly spotted an ocean liner looming directly in front of him. Lee pulled up and climbed to 1,000 feet, then spiraled down and headed for the only flat place he saw, a cemetery. Then a hill suddenly reared up ahead and he had to climb and repeat the process again. This time he came down on a field on Staten Island and smashed into a tree, breaking his wing but escaping injury. "I went right back up the next day," Lee recalled later. "I knew enough not to hesitate, but I was shaking all the way to Washington."

Lee and his fellow airmail pilots were called upon almost daily to demonstrate such resolve, and the young fliers were both comrades and competitors. The Post Office tacitly encouraged the competition by publicly reporting performance statistics. Press releases cited the number of flights started and finished by individual aviators, the number

Proud of their role in the Air Mail Service's first-year achievements, the ground crew at New York's Belmont Park airfield gathers beneath a boastful sign. Posted at the behest of Otto Praeger, the impressive record could be read by passengers riding the nearby Long Island Railroad.

of forced landings and any flights that were notably swift or difficult.

Pilot John Miller, a former naval aviator, was singled out for special praise in March 1919 when he plowed through a blinding snowstorm and 68-mile-per-hour winds before landing safely on Long Island, displaying "courage and successful handling of an aeroplane," the official report said, which have "never been surpassed, perhaps never equalled." Another pilot won a place in airmail annals by sending a perplexing telegram to his backup man after he was compelled to land near the hamlet of North East, Maryland. FORCED DOWN. FOUR MILES SOUTHWEST OF NORTHEAST. SEND HELP, the message read. "That fellow," the confused standby pilot commented, "had better sober up and come home."

By April the Army de Havillands that had failed so conspicuously in their airmail debut in December were back with their modifications completed. The axles and undercarriages had been strengthened to accommodate larger wheels, and the cockpit was relocated to a less perilous position in the rear. Emboldened by the performance of the improved D.H.4s and the arrival of milder weather, the Post Office celebrated the airmail's first anniversary—May 15, 1919—by reinstituting the east-west service that had been so hurriedly abandoned five months before. As a temporary concession to the treacherous Alleghenies, however, the flights were limited to the route between Chicago and Cleveland, with a stop at Bryan, Ohio. During their first week of flying the new route, the pilots completed 28 of their 30 scheduled flights; the two exceptions were cancellations due to high winds. But public support of the new service was less heartening: The first plane to reach Cleveland carried just seven pounds of mail.

Despite widespread indifference, the Air Mail Service carried on, though many pilots were rankled that the bulldog-like Praeger, proud of the airmail record and anxious to firm up his Congressional support, continued to insist that they fly in all but the worst weather. A nonflier himself, he was convinced that a pilot could take off safely in low-visibility conditions if the region he was flying into was reporting clear weather. Praeger's standing directive was: "Fly by compass. Visibility not necessary." The pilots, lacking any direction-finding instruments and knowing that their compasses were undependable, preferred to navigate the only way they could—by keeping the ground in sight.

Friction between the pilots and their superiors intensified after flights between New York and Cleveland—by way of Bellefonte—started on July 1. A spell of rainy and foggy weather resulted in a series of accidents, one of which killed pilot Charles Lamborn near fog-shrouded Bellefonte on July 19. Three days later pilot Windy Smith was ordered to take off on the New York-Washington run in visibility of about 300 feet. His assigned plane was a Curtiss R-4 with a high-compression engine that did not function well at low altitudes. Smith refused.

The Belmont Park field manager asked two other pilots to make the flight, but they also declined. Then he called in Hamilton Lee, who had flown up from Washington the previous day and was due for a layover. When Lee reached Belmont, it was so foggy that he could not even see the race-track grandstands. "My thought was that Windy was a pretty reasonable man and the weather was awful," Lee recalled later, "so I decided to stand behind him." Praeger, learning that two of his star pilots were balking, fired off telegrams dismissing them from the Air Mail Service. For the other fliers, this was the final straw; they informed Praeger that they intended to strike, citing as grievances the summary dismissals of Smith and Lee and what they called "this everlasting 'fly regardless of weather conditions or resign' " policy of the Post Office.

The strike lasted only a day, at the end of which Praeger agreed to confer with a delegation of pilots in Washington. The fliers chose Lee and another airmail pilot, Charles H. Anglin, to represent them, and the two went to the capital. There they met with Praeger to hammer out a new policy on foul-weather flying: A field manager could dispute a pilot's judgment about conditions, but the manager himself would then have to go aloft to determine whether the weather was flyable. The settlement was a compromise, for the final decision rested with the field manager—but at least the judgment would be made by someone at the scene rather than by a deskbound postal official in Washington.

Praeger also agreed to pay the pilots three dollars for each day they spent away from their home base, and to reinstate Hamilton Lee. But there would be no reinstatement for Windy Smith, who had permanently alienated his superiors with a fiery letter to Praeger: "You do not regard a man's life with the least respect," Smith charged in one of his milder accusations. "He stayed fired," Lee recalled long afterward. "He must not have loved flying like I did." ❧

On farmland near Bellefonte, Pennsylvania, a boy watches a man dig through the wreck of Charles Lamborn's de Havilland mailplane. Flying 404 pounds of mail, Lamborn was killed when he slammed into the fogbound hill on July 19, 1919.

"Pony Express with wings"

It was, for Second Assistant Postmaster General Otto Praeger, a "Pony Express with wings," America's first regularly scheduled airmail service between New York, Philadelphia and Washington, D.C. And for the nation, it was a giant step into the Air Age, launched on May 15, 1918, amid all the pomp, patriotic hoopla and expectation pictured here and on the following pages.

But for the Army's Major Reuben H. Fleet, the officer who just eight days before had been put in charge of the fledgling service, getting the mail off the ground was no easy task. Not only did Fleet have to order six modified JN-4Hs from the Curtiss Aeroplane and Motor Company, thus interrupting delivery of trainers to the Army; he had to help put the planes into flying order. The night before they were to take off, four were still being worked on; because of the rush nature of the job, a bottle cork was used to stop a hole in the fuel tank of one.

Nor were these Fleet's only problems. He had to find a suitable New York field for his pilots to use. He got an old friend, Major August Belmont, owner of Belmont Park on Long Island, to lend his race track to the Army. In Washington, he faced a problem of quite another sort. In his words, "a lone, non-symmetrical, ugly and hazardous" tree threatened takeoff and landing at the Polo Grounds *(right)*, the city's temporary field. Fleet asked the Park Commission to cut it down. But when the commission said it would be three months before any action could be taken, Fleet took matters into his own hands and ordered the tree felled, a deed that later brought him criticism from the Secretary of the War Department.

At the Polo Grounds in Washington, Lieutenant George Boyle determinedly awaits the takeoff for Philadelphia on the Air Mail Service's opening day. Beside him, a helpful Major Reuben Fleet bends down to strap an ordinary road map to the flier's knee to assist him in navigating the 140-mile route.

Trees surround the Polo Grounds in Washington's Potomac Park. The Lincoln Memorial is just visible in the photograph's upper right-hand corner.

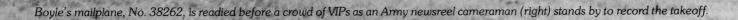

Boyle's mailplane, No. 38262, is readied before a crowd of VIPs as an Army newsreel cameraman (right) stands by to record the takeoff.

Lieutenant Boyle takes off for Philadelphia. When he got lost and landed in Waldorf, Maryland, he came down near Otto Praeger's farm.

Workers at Philadelphia's Bustleton field load the mailplane used by Lieutenant James C. Edgerton to bring the first airmail into Washington, D.C.

A ground crew fuels a specially modified Jenny. Two 19-gallon
fuel tanks gave the planes a range of about 175 miles.

On opening day in New York, a Hamilton Watch Company executive gives Lieutenant Webb a silver timepiece.

Officials load Webb's Jenny with 144 pounds of mail bound for Philadelphia and Washington, as the flier waits in the cockpit.

Amid cheers from the crowd, Webb takes off from Belmont Park, Long Island, with the first airmail from New York.

Seated at the controls before takeoff, Webb radiates confidence for press photographers.

At Bustleton, Philadelphia Postmaster John A. Thornton congratulates airmail pilot James Edgerton just before the final lap to Washington, D.C.

49

Pilot Wesley Smith watches mechanics transfer mail from his D.H.4 to a delivery truck at the Post Office field in Bellefonte, Pennsylvania, a major stopov

...or flights between New York and Cleveland in the 1920s.

2
Uncle Sam's flying postmen

The weather was cloudy and damp as Dean Smith embarked on his first flight across the Allegheny Mountains between Bellefonte, Pennsylvania, and Cleveland, Ohio, in the spring of 1920. Smith had hoped to follow a more experienced pilot in his debut on the rugged route—he had never seen Cleveland, even from the ground—but no seasoned hands were available. As he headed through a gap in the first ridge, he ran into scattered squalls. Zigzagging between the heavy clouds, he had just about cleared the worst of the weather when his engine stopped dead. Beneath him lay a cheerless vista of tree-carpeted hills broken by a single cuplike basin that held a small clearing.

Smith had to swing into a sharp, almost vertical S turn, first left, then right, to reach the clearing without smashing into a cliff. What he did not know was that a three-foot-high ledge, hidden in the brush, was waiting in ambush; as he set the plane down in the clearing, the landing gear slammed into the ledge. "The plane snapped like a popper on the end of a bullwhip," the pilot wrote later. "I was catapulted into a long head-first dive like a man shot from a circus cannon." After rolling over several times in the brush, Smith scrambled to a stop in a sitting position. The padded leather ring that had rimmed the cockpit hung around his neck like a lei, and he was still grasping the rubber grip pulled loose from the control stick. Smith was unhurt, but the wreckage of the de Havilland was "piled in a heap, like crumpled wastepaper," a victim of what pilots came to call the Hell Stretch over the Alleghenies.

The Allegheny Mountains would be among the toughest barriers that faced the fliers of the Air Mail Service. Lacking the dramatic, sky-splitting profile of the Rockies or the Sierra Nevadas, these rolling and humpbacked mountains looked more like a succession of gentle, forested hills. But this was an illusion that had fooled the wagon pioneers of an earlier generation as it now deceived their airborne successors. A mail pilot, forced by the limitations of his equipment to fly by "contact," to navigate by landmarks, realized quickly that these deceptive mountains presented every hazard in the airman's book of horrors—meandering and hard-to-read terrain, sudden and violent changes of weather, thick fog that hid the narrow valleys and curtained the hillsides, and worst of all a shortage of level clearings for the inevitable forced landings.

The Hell Stretch may have been a pilot's hair-raising obstacle course, but the tight-knit little band of fliers, mechanics and clerks assigned to the mountain-ringed field at Bellefonte refused to let the dangers taint their earthly pleasures. Bellefonte, a county-seat town of sturdy frame houses and up-and-down streets surrounded by tidy farms and barns with "Mail Pouch Tobacco" painted on their broad sides, was small enough to appreciate the heroes in its midst. The pilots were feted at parties at the Nittany Country Club and the Brockerhoff House Hotel. In return they staged impromptu air shows for the local citizens. Charles Gates, once a clerk at the field, remembered his job long afterward as "the most exciting work I ever had. We were doing something all the time. There wasn't any time clock." If a plane was late, he recalled, "everyone worried about it. I never saw any group with the camaraderie that we had then."

They were also noted for their spirited high jinks, as freshly hired rookie James H. "Jack" Knight discovered when he flew into Bellefonte one summer afternoon in 1919. Learning that the young pilot was a newlywed, the ground crew dressed a mechanic in a bridal gown and drove Knight and his surrogate bride around Bellefonte in a truck decorated with bells, old shoes, tin cans and the tail section of a wrecked mailplane. Harold T. "Slim" Lewis, regarded by many of his peers as the best flier in the mail service, sometimes flew so low over the courthouse on High Street that the fish-shaped weather vane atop the building would spin in his prop wash. And, Gates recalled, pilot William Hopson once needed to get to New York so urgently, for romantic reasons, that he hitched a ride with another pilot; since the mail compartment was already full, Hopson "got onto the wing, lay up against the fuselage and held onto the guy wires all the way."

For all the formidable hazards of the Hell Stretch, fatalism seemed foreign to the high-spirited fliers' nature. "None of them ever thought their number would come up," Gates declared. "You couldn't get a pilot to think that. If they thought that they would have quit."

The Post Office Department was fortunate to have such a crop of optimistic pilots. For the two years beginning in mid-1919 were a kind of crucible for the fledgling Air Mail Service, a time when Second Assistant Postmaster General Otto Praeger and his deputies seemed to reel from crisis to crisis like deck officers on a storm-bullied ship. Their troubles were both internal and external. Eager as always to demonstrate airmail's feasibility, postal officials added new routes and fields, experimented with new planes and hired new pilots, but their reach often exceeded their grasp. Sometimes it was the pilots that failed and sometimes the planes; other times the weather sabotaged both pilot and plane. But often the plans simply exceeded the available resources, and skeptical congressmen, viewing the Air Mail Service's fire-and-fall-back performance with the eyes of nervous loan officers, threatened repeatedly to cut off its funds.

They had ample reason for their concern. At the end of 1919

The gently rolling contours of the Allegheny Mountains belie the treacherous flying conditions that led airmail pilots of the 1920s to call the region the Hell Stretch. More fatal accidents occurred in this area than on any other part of the transcontinental route.

there were still only two regular routes, New York-Washington (the Philadelphia stop had been abandoned as unnecessary after the acquisition of longer-range de Havillands) and New York-Chicago via Bellefonte and Cleveland. Washington operations had been shifted from the temporary field on the Polo Grounds to a proper airstrip at College Park, Maryland, and the New York terminal had been moved from the temporary facilities at Belmont Park race track to Heller Field in Newark, New Jersey. But Heller was little more than a runway hemmed in by a canal, two sets of railroad tracks and the Tiffany jewelry factory. Mail was still carried by plane only during daylight hours.

The single-engined de Havillands acquired from the Army and rebuilt to postal specifications were still the workhorses of the service, supplemented by a few Curtiss R-4s and two other planes that the mailmen were just beginning to try—modified twin-engined Martin bombers, and de Havillands that had been converted to twin-engined planes by the installation of a pair of six-cylinder engines in place of the 12-cylinder Liberty. With this mixed fleet of aircraft the nation's aerial mailmen made their appointed rounds.

In January 1921 Praeger wrote: "There is hardly a day passes, that some pilot does not have a thrilling experience in getting the

Bystanders mill around the wreckage of Harry Sherlock's D.H.4 after the plane struck the chimney of the Tiffany jewelry plant in Newark, New Jersey, while approaching the adjacent airfield in 1920. Sherlock was killed and the field was later closed because of the many dangerous obstructions around its runway.

mail through to its destination." Praeger's observation was accurate enough, but the boastful tone could not quite hide an unpleasant statistic: Twenty-six Air Mail Service employees died in crashes between October 1919 and July 1921, an average of more than one a month. Of the 19 who were pilots, none fell so swiftly as 24-year-old John P. Charlton Jr., who made his debut as a mail pilot on an October morning in 1919 and was killed when his plane plowed into a fog-veiled New Jersey hillside two days later. Pilot Harry Sherlock died in March 1920 when his de Havilland clipped a brick chimney on the Tiffany factory adjoining Heller Field. Only 12 days afterward a clerk at Heller, joy-riding with pilot Frederick Robinson in a Curtiss Jenny, was crushed to death when the craft went into a sudden spin and plummeted 1,000 feet to the ground. Robinson survived, only to die five months later when his plane smashed into a rocky stream bed near Millersburg, Pennsylvania.

Praeger, in the meantime, had continued his tireless campaign for new mail routes, zeroing in on Omaha as the logical next stop on the airmail's inexorable progression toward the west. His goal, of course, was a continuous route between the Atlantic and the Pacific Oceans, a tantalizing possibility that seemed even more feasible after a contingent of Army pilots completed a coast-to-coast round-trip race in October 1919.

Service between Chicago and Omaha was launched with suitable fanfare on the winter morning of January 8, 1920, only to cease with minimal explanation a day later. But Praeger's plans finally began to fall into place in May, when Chicago-Omaha flights were resumed and operated on a regular basis. Throughout the remainder of 1920 the westering impulse was in full cry: A Post Office representative went on the road to persuade the cities along the projected route—North Platte, Nebraska; Cheyenne and Rock Springs, Wyoming; Salt Lake City; Elko and Reno, Nevada; and San Francisco—to provide hangars and airstrips. A Chicago-St. Louis feeder route (so called

Frederick A. Robinson's plane lies on its back in the Susquehanna River near Millersburg, Pennsylvania, in 1920. Robinson was flying low through mist on the New York-to-Cleveland run when his landing gear hit a cable strung across the water; the plane flipped over and crashed, instantly killing him.

because it was tangential to the main east-west airway) commenced in August. And then, in the following month, postal pilot Randolph G. Page set out on the first leg of the long-awaited inaugural coast-to-coast mail flight.

Page lifted his de Havilland off from Hazelhurst Field on Long Island (Heller had recently been forsaken as too small) shortly before 7 a.m. on September 8, refueled at Bellefonte and Cleveland and then flew on to Chicago, where he turned the mail over to James P. Murray, an American pilot who had flown for Britain's Royal Flying Corps during World War I. Murray made it to Iowa City by nightfall but was delayed for several hours the next morning by fog. Taking off at 10:15, he stopped for fuel at Omaha and North Platte and touched down at Cheyenne at dusk. On the following day he battled head winds en route to Rock Springs, flew over the Rockies at an altitude of between 12,000 and 14,000 feet and pulled into Salt Lake City, where pilot John Woodward was waiting, at midday.

Woodward, hoping to reach Reno by dark, had to wait out an exuberant and extended civic celebration before he could leave Salt Lake City, and then he ran into fierce head winds over the high desert. Forced to come down at Lovelock, Nevada, 100 miles short of Reno, Woodward was injured while making a difficult landing on a small field; Edison Mouton was sent from Reno to relieve him. Mouton flew the final leg into San Francisco's Marina Field, landing at 2:20 p.m. on September 11 before a cluster of waiting dignitaries and movie cameramen. The actual flying time for the historic flight was 34 hours and 5 minutes; total elapsed time, including the hours lost to darkness, fog, wind and enthusiastic mail recipients, was 75 hours and 52 minutes, beating the best railroad time by 22 hours. The pilots of the Air Mail Service could still take to the air safely only during daylight, but they had staged a dramatic demonstration of airmail's long-distance potential.

The beginning of transcontinental flights brought new excitement to the cities and towns along the way and boosted the morale of the pilots. The first arrival in any town of an inelegant but sturdy de Havilland biplane with "U.S. MAIL" emblazoned on its fuselage was a genuine sensation. In the West a mail pilot might still be regarded as a hero dropped from the empty sky, an instant flesh-and-blood link with family back East, a daredevil who braved mountains and deserts to get the mail through. Dean Smith, ferrying a plane west before the service actually began, found that "everyplace we landed—Cheyenne, North Platte, Rock Springs—our arrival was a civic occasion" with speeches and banquets and testaments of praise and gratitude. Even in the jaded East the idea of a chain of planes spanning the continent, conquering in a little more than three days the vastness that had taken the Forty-Niners four and five months to cross, could still seize the imagination. It was, in spite of everything, a bold and romantic notion, and a few days after the first California-bound mail was committed to the air a con-

A haven on the Hell Stretch

When the Post Office decided, in the summer of 1918, to establish airmail service between New York and Cleveland, it sent veteran pilot Max Miller to reconnoiter a site for a fuel stop. Miller picked a farmer's field near Bellefonte, Pennsylvania, and the following year the first westbound mail flight touched down on the town's new landing strip.

It was a boon that made Bellefonte the envy of its neighbors—particularly those of Lock Haven, who had hoped the airport would be located there—and for the next seven years the town provided a lively stop for the daring pilots flying mail over the razor-backed Alleghenies. In 1920 the tiny airport became one of the country's first radio-equipped fields and its future seemed assured.

But by the mid-1920s the town's star was in decline as newer, longer-range planes replaced the Post Office's aging D.H.4s. The Post Office shut down the field in 1926, marking the end of an era for the airmail as well as for Bellefonte.

A buggy rolls past the Brockerhoff House Hotel, where most of the mail pilots laying over in Bellefonte stayed during the 1920s.

A white circle marks the Bellefonte field with its hangar and its repair shop (inset).

The airfield's original wooden hangars (above) were destroyed by fire in 1919. All-metal structures replaced them the following year.

tributor to *The New York Times* captured the feeling in this salute:

> There's a speck in the sky and a drone on the wind,
> A sound as of harpstrings and drums.
> With its struts and its wires humming sweetly in tune,
> In the path of the eagles it comes.
> A man-made and marvelous bird of the air,
> The century's glory and boast,
> The plane, that through cloudland triumphantly bears
> Aerial mail to the coast.

The pilots who flew west of Cheyenne during that first fall and winter of the transcontinental operation must have chuckled at such poesy, for they knew that they could expect a new and perilous adventure almost daily. Out of Cheyenne they ran into the jagged Laramie and Medicine Bow Mountains, which they dubbed the Hump. Farther west lay the Continental Divide and the 11,000-foot-high peaks of the Wasatch Range just east of Salt Lake City. From there it was desert and barren hills until they encountered the formidable Ruby Mountains in eastern Nevada, then the empty, sage-flecked expanse of Nevada and finally the granite spires of the Sierra. Wherever possible the route was laid out close to the railroad tracks, which not only pointed the way east and west but offered the most likely means of finding help in case of a crash or forced landing. And the pilots soon realized that the Rockies had at least one vital aeronautical asset that the Alleghenies lacked: Because of their sheer immensity, their high valleys and plateaus were correspondingly larger, providing better sites for emergency landings.

Jimmy Murray, who had flown the longest leg of the first coast-to-coast flight, was caught in a blizzard between Salt Lake City and Cheyenne in October. Trapped below the high peaks with only a seamless wall of white visible in front of him, he crash-landed on the side of a mountain. Finding himself unhurt, Murray spent a cold and hungry night on the shore of a high-country lake and tramped 17 miles through the snow the next day to reach a village. The men sent out to retrieve the mail found the plane with the aid of tracks left by a bear that had trailed the pilot on his trek. Three weeks later John Woodward, another of the four men on the inaugural cross-country trip, was not so lucky. Overtaken by fog as he tried to negotiate the Hump, Woodward was killed when he crashed in the foothills of the Laramie Mountains.

Freelance journalist John Goldstrom experienced the full range of obstacles that the West presented to mailplanes when he had himself appointed a special postal agent and hitched a ride across the country in late 1920. In the East, his major discomforts were caused by the arctic chill and bouts of airsickness, but the ride west of Omaha was enlivened by five forced landings, two of them due to mechanical failures and the other three to stormy weather. In Nevada he and pilot Edison Mouton were driven to the ground by a dust storm so severe that they had to wait four hours before they could see well enough to leave the plane. After

James Murray, whose 1,300-mile flight from Chicago to Salt Lake City in 1920 helped establish the first transcontinental airmail route, was a former schoolteacher who learned to fly in World War I. Studying law in his spare time, he went on to become vice president of the Boeing Airplane Company.

that, they set out on an all-night 25-mile hike to the nearest ranch, an ordeal that convinced Goldstrom that "a lot of shoe leather can be worn out in cross-country flying."

When he finally landed in San Francisco, 13 days after he had left New York, Goldstrom had a new and hard-won respect for mail pilots. "I have sat at many an aeronautical banquet," he wrote later, "and heard high praise heaped upon the heads of this or that politically appointed official under whose administration the air mail advanced and became successful, but I have joined in the applause only when the speaker got around to mentioning the pilots."

The preoccupation with westward expansion had been accompanied by an equally intense quest for new and better planes for the mail pilots. Neither the Martin bombers nor the twin de Havillands had performed adequately—primarily because their load-carrying capacity declined sharply when one engine failed—but postal officials had high hopes for the German-made Junkers F 13s that appeared in the United States in mid-1920. Imported by aviation promoter John M. Larsen and renamed the J.L. 6, the craft was radical in every respect: A single-engined, all-metal monoplane, it was strong enough to carry a 1,000-pound load with an engine of only 185 horsepower. Moreover, it could cruise for six to seven hours on low-grade fuel—the de Havilland, by contrast, required a 400-horsepower engine to carry just 400 pounds and could cruise only three hours, on high-test fuel. Postmaster General Albert Burleson, hoping to cut operating costs by as much as 50 per cent, bought eight of the German miracle planes and ordered them into service after a coast-to-coast test flight in July and August.

A few days later pilot Wesley Smith, carrying the mail and one crewman, was flying a J.L. 6 from Chicago to New York when the engine

Officials inspect a German-built Junkers F 13 transport plane imported by businessman John Larsen and sold in America as the J.L. 6. In 1920 the Air Mail Service bought eight Junkers for $20,000 each and put them into service on the route between New York, Chicago and Omaha.

suddenly fell silent. Smith looked down at the floor of the cockpit and was horrified to see bright fingers of flame clutching at his ankles. The fire climbed the left side of the enclosed pilot's compartment and threatened the fuel tanks. Smith confronted an aviator's nightmare—a mid-air fire with the danger of explosion increasing by the minute. He threw the burning plane into a sideslip, diving broadside-first in hopes that the wind would put out the flames. The altimeter fell lower and lower as he plunged sideways toward the ground. Gradually the flames receded, then subsided altogether.

Smith's desperate strategy had worked, but he had lost valuable altitude and, with his engine out, was still dropping. Spiraling to slow his descent, he brought the ship down in a cornfield. Smith and his crewman, both of them suffering minor burns, leaped from the plane before it stopped and hit the ground running.

On the next day, September 1, the first civilian airmail pilot, Max Miller—who had rejoined the postal service not long after quitting to protest Ben Lipsner's departure in late 1918—eased another J.L. 6 off the runway at Hazelhurst en route to Chicago. Beside him was mechanic Gustav Rierson. Miller was a classic contact flier who preferred to operate at low altitudes, navigating by terrain features. He and Rierson had reached the vicinity of Morristown, New Jersey, when witnesses on the ground noticed the plane backfiring, moving erratically and losing altitude at about 1,000 feet. Miller was too low to sideslip. Seconds later the J.L. 6 plunged to earth with flames trailing behind. It exploded as it struck the ground, killing both men instantly.

The public was stunned by Miller's death and by the J.L. 6's puzzling performance. "Premier Mail Pilot Dies in Flaming Fall," *The New York Times* headlined, and the odd fact that Miller and Rierson had gone only

45 miles in the two and a half hours before they crashed led to speculation that the cause of the accident was human and not mechanical. Miller had complained of feeling ill shortly before takeoff; some thought he had become incapacitated in the cockpit and that the inexperienced Rierson had been flying the plane when it ran into trouble. But the J.L. 6's mid-air failures were alarmingly persistent; Dean Smith reported that he had to make 16 successive dead-stick landings in the planes. "I'd hear a sound like a giant sledge hammer hitting the bottom of the plane," he said, "and I'd start looking for a good place to come down."

Not all pilots were as fortunate as Smith. Thirteen days after Miller's fatal flight, pilot Walter Stevens—who was on his last mail run before taking a job with the Glenn L. Martin Company in Cleveland—was winging over the countryside near Pemberville, Ohio, when observers on the ground heard a loud noise from his plane. Stevens, a popular veteran who had performed exhibition flights for the townsfolk in Bellefonte, managed to nurse the J.L. 6 into a landing pattern at the first sign of trouble, but as he eased the craft down on a farm field the fuel tank blew up, killing Stevens and his mechanic, Russell Thomas.

Mechanics at the Bellefonte airstrip work a hand-operated pump to refuel a J.L. 6. The plane's design represented a significant step forward in aircraft construction techniques: Fuselage, wings and skin were all made of metal.

The similarities in the accidents eliminated any doubt that the fault lay with the plane and not with the pilots. Recoiling from the onslaught of editorial criticism precipitated by four deaths in two weeks—the *New York Sun* labeled the airmail a deadly fad—the Post Office pulled the remaining J.L. 6s off the line and turned them over to the mechanics. A thorough inspection pinpointed a rigid fuel line as the principal villain: The metal line cracked when it vibrated in flight, spewing out fuel that caught fire when the engine backfired. The mechanics installed a flexible hose connection to eliminate the leaks caused by vibration; other changes were designed to drain the fuel that accumulated in the fuselage beneath the engine. Praeger, thrown on the defensive, argued that "the comparatively few casualties in the air-mail service justify the splendid work that the air mail is doing," but Dean Smith and others continued to have doubts. "The air mail was run by people who knew nothing about aviation," Smith declared later, "and it never changed."

Reluctant to abandon a plane that promised a longer cruising range and cheaper operating costs at a time of ever-expanding routes, the Post Office restored the J.L. 6 to duty in late 1920. But in February 1921 a third fatal crash ended the craft's violent career as a mail-plane. Making its initial foray on the Chicago-Minneapolis feeder route that had been established the previous November, a J.L. 6 crewed by pilots William M. Carroll and Hiram H. Rowe and mechanic Robert B. Hill fell to earth at La Crosse, Wisconsin, under eerily familiar circumstances. "There was a flash," the Chicago *Tribune* reported, "a burst of flame, then a terrific explosion." The plane "crumpled and fell wing over wing" for 600 feet. A formal board of inquiry, convened in response to Congressional insistence, determined that a backfire had ignited loose fuel in the engine compartment. The board recommended that the J.L. 6 be withdrawn once again, and this time the miracle plane was out for good.

Faulty aircraft were not the only problems dogging the airmail. With a new Republican administration set to take office and Democratic appointees like Burleson and Praeger facing unemployment, the Air Mail Service they had built and boosted was under siege from several directions. Anti-airmail congressmen, who had almost managed to eliminate the service's appropriation a year earlier, corraled enough votes to cut the $1.25 million allotted to the airmail from the Post Office budget. The spectacular failure of the Junkers squelched the enthusiasm of press and public, and an independent investigation authorized by Congress uncovered sloppy maintenance practices and recurrent late or incompleted flights.

The investigators discovered that the record on the Hell Stretch run between New York and Cleveland was particularly dreary. In the last nine months of 1920, only 55 per cent of the scheduled Cleveland-to-New York flights had actually been completed. The mail carried on those flights arrived at its destination an average of 3 hours and 33 minutes behind schedule, which meant that it was barely beating train-borne letters. The probers also attacked the Air Mail Service's own buoyant statistics as a public relations ploy based on estimates that often had "little or no foundation."

Much of the criticism was true, and the single all-embracing explanation for the airmail's numerous failings was haste. Pilots and mechanics had been hastily hired and trained, routes hastily laid out, planes hastily tested and sometimes hastily serviced. A thin line of mailplanes had been deployed across the nation before the system had settled into an efficient and dependable pattern. Overanxious to justify itself to Congress and the business community and thus to guarantee its future, the Air Mail Service had taken on too much too soon.

For all its shortcomings, however, the airmail's achievements had gained it an impressive corps of defenders. President Woodrow Wilson, soon to be replaced by Warren G. Harding, endorsed the conclusion reached by the National Advisory Committee for Aeronautics, that the service was "in effect an experimental laboratory for the development of the civil uses of aircraft" and for that reason alone was "worth what it costs over and above the value of the service it actually renders in the more rapid transportation of mail." The loyalists in the press were even more ardent. "The same objections now being brought out against the air mail," the Omaha *Bee* editorialized, "were once used in argument against rural free delivery, the postal savings bank and the parcel post." The magazine *Outlook* declared: "The country not only *can* afford its air mail, it *must* afford it. If there are unusual dangers involved in the air mail, it is not the part of courage or intelligence to drop the service on that account. The challenge to us is not to eliminate the dangers by leaving the air, but by fully conquering it."

Praeger and his Post Office colleagues had no intention of abandoning the service, and on February 21, 1921, a short back-page news item from Omaha contained the first hint of how they planned to revive the airmail's drooping reputation while simultaneously advancing toward the full conquest of the air. The story said that planes would leave San Francisco and New York the next morning—two from each direction—in an unprecedented attempt to make continuous day-and-night flights across the country. Townsfolk along the way had agreed to light bonfires to help mark the route, and postal officials hoped that the coast-to-coast flights could be made in fewer than 36 hours.

As a political move the idea was a potential master stroke: Congress, by no coincidence, was due to vote that week on the airmail appropriation—which the Senate had restored. The drama of a night flight across the Great Plains was bound to captivate congressmen and ordinary folk alike. Thirty-six-hour transcontinental mail delivery would be Otto Praeger's legacy to the incoming Republicans and the country. Round-the-clock flights would at last demonstrate the airmail's clear-cut advantage over surface mail and make it possible for business concerns to save critical time in transactions between major financial centers. But the timing of the first flights, dictated by politics, could hardly have been worse for the pilots. They would be contending with short days, the risk of blizzards and midwinter temperatures—in addition to a virtually unlighted airway.

Elmer V. Leonhardt and Ernest M. Allison, the pilots from the East, took off from Hazelhurst Field a little after 6:00 a.m. on February 22 and soon were droning through chill winds toward their first stop, Bellefonte. About an hour and a half later, pilots Farr Nutter and Ray Little lifted their de Havillands over San Francisco and headed for the Sacramento Valley and the High Sierra, climbing to 18,000 feet as they crossed the snow-crowned mountains at dawn. At Reno, Nutter turned his mail pouches over to Jack Eaton; Little gave way to William Lewis, who was enjoying his last month as a bachelor before a scheduled March wedding. The change of planes and pilots at Reno took only 10 minutes.

Flying into the rising sun, Eaton and Lewis followed the railroad tracks across the Great Basin country to Elko, landing six minutes apart. Eaton was off again for Salt Lake City at 9:31, after spending only seven minutes on the ground. Lewis was airborne a few moments later, but his plane stalled as he climbed out of Elko, then plunged to earth. The pilot was dead when the ground crew reached him.

Leonhardt and Allison meanwhile had come in over Nittany Mountain to the little field at Bellefonte, refueled and set off across the Hell Stretch in a thickening mist. Leonhardt, flying in the lead, was forced down by the weather soon afterward near Du Bois, Pennsylvania, but

Minneapolis postal workers display delivery trucks advertising the new airmail service, begun after local businessmen persuaded the Post Office to open a route between Chicago and Minneapolis in 1920. Lack of patronage ended the service 18 months later.

Seven of the pilots who flew airmail on the short-lived Chicago-Twin Cities route cluster around E. Hamilton Lee's de Havilland at the Minneapolis Speedway in 1920. Lee, wearing a cap, is at left perched atop the nose of the plane.

Allison fought his way through to Cleveland and tranferred his load of mail to Wesley Smith's plane. Smith flew on to Chicago, arriving at 3:10 p.m., but a storm front was bearing down on the city. Dean Smith and Bill Hopson, the pilot who once rode on a wing from Bellefonte to New York, were standing by at Chicago's Checkerboard Field to fly the next lap to Omaha. Heavy snow was falling when Hopson went up with Wesley Smith's mailbags; 10 minutes later, Hopson returned to the field and reported that there was no way a plane could beat its way through the storm. With no indication of a break in the weather, the night's westbound flights were officially canceled.

Now it was up to the men flying eastward. Jack Eaton, unaware that Lewis had crashed behind him at Elko, droned over the 11,400-foot-high Ruby Mountains and landed at Salt Lake City at 11:30 a.m. Crewmen in Elko had meanwhile recovered the mail from Lewis' wrecked de Havilland and loaded it in a plane piloted by William F. Blanchfield, who took off after a two-hour delay.

The white towers of the Wasatch Range glistened in the midday sun as Jimmy Murray, the flier who had been tracked by a bear a few months earlier, took the relay from Eaton in Salt Lake City. Murray had been flying the high country all winter, and he cruised easily over the Continental Divide and across the rugged Medicine Bow and Laramie Mountains. He touched down in Cheyenne a little before 5 o'clock; Frank Yager took off five minutes later on the run over the prairie to North Platte, Nebraska. The weather was still clear, but darkness descended as Yager neared his goal. The field crew at North Platte ignited a bucket of gasoline to give him enough light for landing. The second eastbound plane, now in the hands of pilot Harry G. Smith—the Air Mail Service was overloaded with Smiths, all of them unrelated—touched down at North Platte an hour later.

The next lap, from North Platte to Omaha, would be the first real test of the feasibility of nighttime flying over an unmarked route. Praeger and Burleson had already talked of beginning daily day-and-night flights in the spring; the pilots would fly at night by their compasses and drop flares when they needed a visual fix. Jack Knight, who earlier that day had flown his regular Omaha-to-Cheyenne route and then deadheaded back to North Platte, had drawn the first-section night flight to Omaha. Knight, recognized as one of the finest airmail pilots, was scheduled to fly the same plane that Yager had brought in, but Yager broke a tail skid in landing. Mechanics got to work repairing it. Harry Smith meantime ascended into the blackness and flew on to Omaha.

It was 10:44 p.m. by the time the skid was repaired and Knight could finally take off. A layer of clouds obscured the moon as he climbed to 2,200 feet and leveled off above the dim silver strand of the Platte River. The glow of huge bonfires in the river towns of Lexington, Kearney and Grand Island told him that he was on course. Forty miles out of Omaha he saw the lights of the city, then spotted a U-shaped row of red lights marking the landing strip. Thinking about the good meal and warm bed that awaited him, he gunned his engine to announce his arrival and dropped down onto the Omaha field, where a crowd of some 2,000 people watched him land. It was 1:10 a.m., February 23.

Field manager William Votaw greeted Knight with a litany of bad news: The pilot who was due to relieve him was still weathered in at Chicago; Harry Smith had landed in Omaha and stopped for the night; snow was predicted along the 432-mile route across Iowa and Illinois to Chicago. Praeger's farewell coup was in danger of collapsing, and the completion of this daring mission—and possibly the future of the airmail itself—depended on one tired man in a fur-lined flying suit. Votaw could not order him to fly; it was up to Knight. He said he would go.

What he needed, he told Votaw, was a map, for he had never flown the Omaha-to-Chicago route before, even in daylight. All Votaw had was a road map. Knight ripped out the Omaha-Chicago section and put it in his pocket, then climbed into his plane and took off. Now the newspapers were belatedly recognizing a dramatic story. A bulletin in the final edition of the Chicago *Tribune* reported that "Pilot Jack Knight hopped off at 2 o'clock this morning enroute for Chicago."

Flying east over Iowa in fair visibility, Knight followed a compass

course for Des Moines that allowed for a 25-mile-an-hour north wind.
He soon spotted the lighted dome of the Iowa state capitol. "I was fairly
dead for lack of sleep," he told a reporter later. "I was constantly on the
verge of dozing. I gripped the control stick with my knees and began
slapping my hands together. Then I tried to arouse myself by hammer-
ing my own face." Twenty miles past Des Moines a snowstorm snapped
him to alertness. The snow blotted out his horizon and forced him to dip
lower and lower until he skimmed the treetops. About 15 miles west of
Iowa City he sighted a railroad and followed it until he saw the town.

Running short of both fuel and oil, Knight circled the sleeping town
for about 12 minutes in a vain search for the airfield. The ground crew,
believing that all flights for the night had been canceled, had gone
home, but a watchman finally touched off a flare that enabled the pilot
to see just enough to make a nearly perfect landing at 4:45 a.m. The
crewmen, roused by the whine of his engine, showed up to service the
plane while Knight telephoned Chicago and munched a sandwich.

Knight napped fitfully as he waited for a break in the clouds over Iowa
City. Then at 6:30 he took off on the last 200-mile stretch. Steering
northeast as the first shafts of light crept over the horizon, he began to
see lantern-toting farmers doing their morning chores. Now, with the
night and the snow both behind him, he was sure that he would make it.
Checking his road map, he began to pick up landmarks on the outskirts
of Chicago. Just as he reached the city his engine sputtered ominously,

but Knight was so close now that he could almost glide to the ground.

The crewmen in Chicago, who had kept flares burning for him through the night, saw Knight circle the field twice and then ease down to a perfect landing at 8:40. Photographers and reporters who had waited for several hours swarmed around him as the crew transferred the mail to a plane piloted by Jack Webster.

Webster took off for Cleveland while an exhausted Knight tried to cope with the demands of celebrity. He was an instant hero, the airmail's first, and he handled it with the modesty that Americans love. Why was his nose encased in adhesive plaster? a reporter asked. A week earlier, Knight explained, he had broken the nose, his plane and a couple of pine trees when he crashed in Wyoming's Laramie Mountains. "Then I found a town and went back to work." How did he feel now? another newsman queried. "Fine, except that I need some eats and some sleep." What about the flight from Omaha? "I got tangled up in the fog and snow a little bit," he said. "Once or twice I had to go down and mow some trees to find out where I was, but it did not amount to much." His most worrisome moments, he confessed, came when he was trying "to find Iowa City on a dark night with a good snow and fog hanging around. Finding Chicago—why that was a cinch."

As headline writers searched for superlatives to describe Knight's great flight ("Conquest of the Air," "Jack Knight, Ace of the Air Mail Service, Hailed"), Webster sped on to Cleveland and passed the postal torch to Ernest Allison, who flew the last leg over the Hell Stretch to New York. He arrived at Hazelhurst Field at 4:50 p.m. on the 23rd—33 hours and 20 minutes after Farr Nutter had left San Francisco. The time was some 65 hours faster than the best train time, and Praeger could hardly contain himself. The coast-to-coast flight was "the most momentous step in civil aviation," he exclaimed, a "demonstration of the entire feasibility of commercial night flying." It would revolutionize postal operations worldwide. Congress, as intended, got the message: The next day the Air Mail Service's $1.25 million appropriation was approved by nearly a 2-to-1 vote. 〰

The wreckage of a D.H.4 mailplane lies strewn about the Chicago cemetery where pilot Bryan McMullen crashed while attempting to land at the nearby airfield in 1920. McMullen escaped injury but was killed two weeks later on a flight to Omaha when his plane crashed in the fog and burned.

A war veteran's new lease on life

The offer was simply too good to refuse. The Army would turn over to the postal service 100 surplus World War I de Havillands, complete with spare parts and extra Liberty engines, that could be used to fly the mail. But there was a catch: The D.H.4s had severe limitations as mail carriers.

The problems with the British-designed D.H.4 were traceable to its military origins. As a bomber and a reconnaissance plane, it had been used mainly for short flights at high altitudes—not for the long-distance, low-altitude hauls that were the mailplane's stock in trade. Worse, the D.H.4 was lightly constructed; its builders had not anticipated a protracted lifespan for the plane. The onetime bomber was neither strong enough to carry a heavy mail load nor reliable enough to fly on a tight schedule.

The Air Mail Service hired four aircraft firms to work out design modifications and then set up its own refitting shops to make over the D.H.4s. At these depots the planes—many of which arrived in their wartime shipping crates—were rebuilt from the ground up.

The fabric cover gave way to a birch plywood skin that acted as reinforcement. The original plane had two cockpits—a forward one for the pilot and another for a gunner. In the conversion the pilot's station became a mail compartment and the gunner's position was remodeled into a full-fledged cockpit. A conventional control stick, favored by the pilots, replaced the wheel-type control column. The wooden prop was metal tipped to prevent damage to the blades. The Liberty engines were stripped and given new piston rings, bearings and heavy stub-toothed gears, thus ensuring more efficiency and reducing the frequency of engine failures that had plagued the Army planes.

The effort paid off: For almost eight years the D.H.4 served as the workhorse of the Air Mail Service. And the pilots who flew it, many of whom went on to become airline captains, never lost their warm affection for the old plane.

Midway through its refitting at the postal service's Hazelhurst, Long Island, shop, the twin-cockpit D.H.4 has become a single-seater with a 400-pound mail capacity. Behind it is another World War I aircraft, a Curtiss Jenny. (The background decoration on these pages consists of detailed drawings of the original D.H.4 design.)

19-11 11/16

MACHINE GUN SIGHT   DOUBLE FLYING WIRES
FIXED VICKERS 30 CAL. M.G.   SINGLE LANDING WIRE

UPPER
& TAIL
OF WINGS

ELAGE

KID

ED M.G.

LENGTH

2-A

LENGTH

BOTH ROLLS-ROYCE & LIBERTY MODELS HAD THE
OPTIONAL SEATING ARRANGEMENTS. ALL
LIBERTY MODELS HAD MODIFIED REAR

'DEH-4' WITH 300 H.P. MODEL "H" HISPANO-SUIZA ENGINE
(8'6" DIA. TWO BLADED SQUARE TIPPED PROPELLER)

71

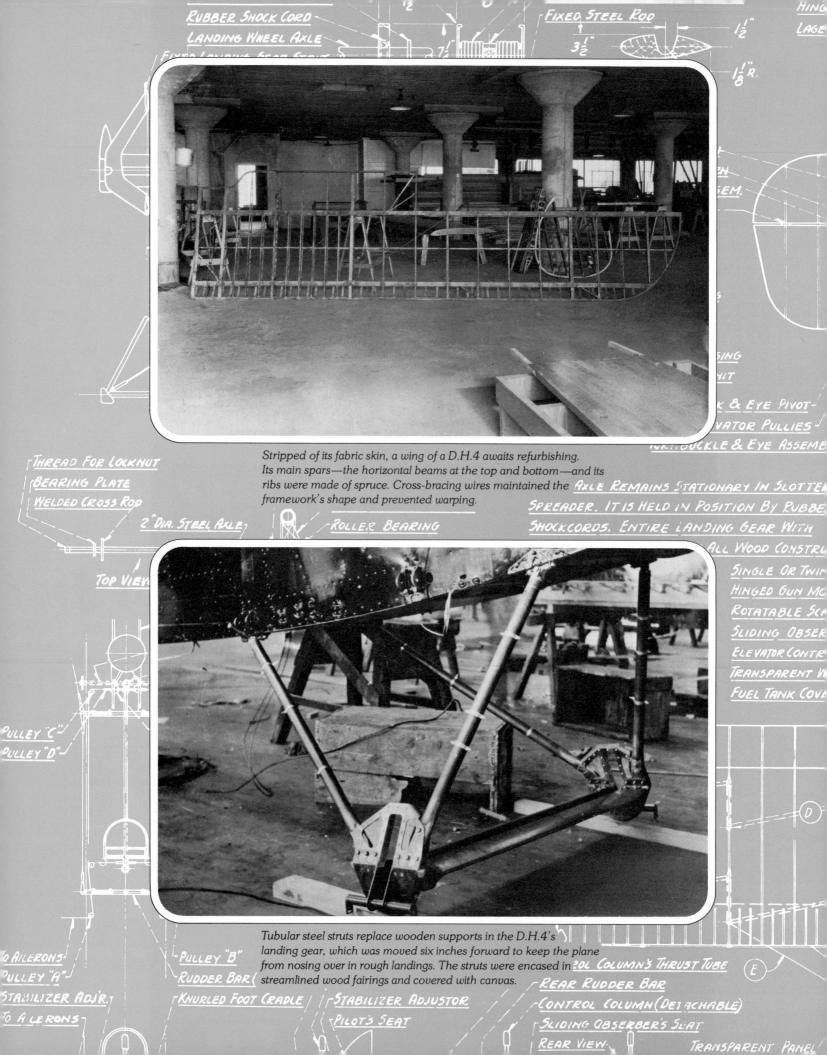

Stripped of its fabric skin, a wing of a D.H.4 awaits refurbishing. Its main spars—the horizontal beams at the top and bottom—and its ribs were made of spruce. Cross-bracing wires maintained the framework's shape and prevented warping.

Tubular steel struts replace wooden supports in the D.H.4's landing gear, which was moved six inches forward to keep the plane from nosing over in rough landings. The struts were encased in streamlined wood fairings and covered with canvas.

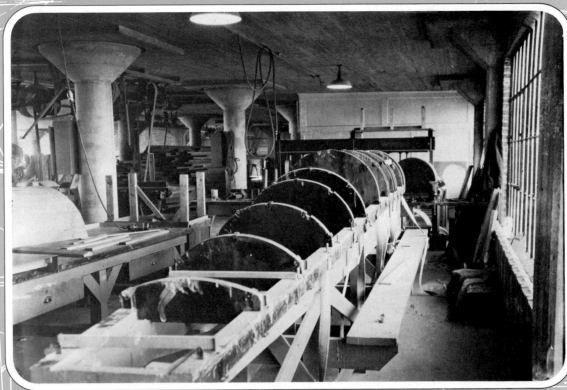

To build standardized tops for the new single-cockpit D.H.4s, refitters at Maywood Field used this jig as a mold. The framework and sheathing for the turtleback were shaped to the jig's contours, then lifted away as a unit and attached to the top of the fuselage.

Mechanics at Maywood display the test stands they used to evaluate engine performance. Though the Liberty engines mounted on the stands were the most reliable motors of their time, they had to be overhauled after every 150 hours aloft.

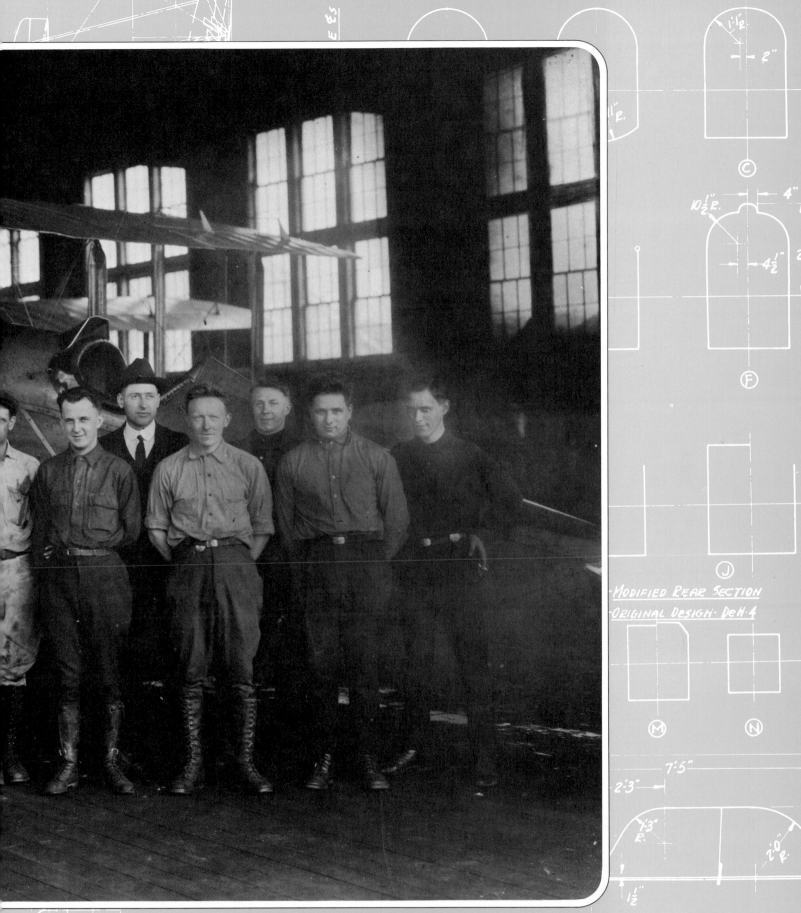

The ground crew at Hazelhurst assembles in front of a rebuilt
de Havilland. The exhaust stack, seen behind the hatted man on the
left, was extended to keep its glow from blinding pilots at night.

MODIFIED REAR SECTION
ORIGINAL DESIGN- DeH-4

A 500,000,000-candlepower beacon and a landing light illuminate a D.H.4 at Omaha's airfield, where a crowd has gathered to watch the departure o

3

Daring the impossible

resident Warren G. Harding, his Republican administration and the elusive mood he called "normalcy" arrived in Washington on March 4, 1921, only nine days after Jack Knight's pioneering all-night flight over the American midlands. What normalcy meant for the United States Air Mail Service became obvious at once: across-the-board cuts, a rollback from Otto Praeger's aggressive and expansive policies, and a general lowering of the postal voice.

The days when Post Office hotspurs would rush to fly every route that looked promising were officially over; the new words to fly by, as spoken by incoming Postmaster General Will H. Hays and his deputy, Edward H. Shaughnessy, who inherited Praeger's job, were "practical," "efficient" and "safe." "We don't want spectacular performances simply because they attract attention," Hays said in a not-too-subtle reference to Knight's one-shot feat. The Post Office would halt the "too rapid expansion" of service, Shaughnessy added, and concentrate on "standardizing and perfecting the operation on a more restricted route."

The Air Mail Service was, in fact, in sore need of such redirection. Praeger's energetic leadership may have produced a string of impressive achievements, but it had also put considerable strain on the service's fleet of planes, on its pilots and ground crews, and on the sympathies of congressmen who doled out all-important funding.

As soon as they were comfortably settled at their new desks, the fresh appointees at the Post Office began to reorganize and streamline the nation's airmail system. From the start, they determined to concentrate on establishing regular service from coast to coast, and to scrap all the routes tangential to the New York-San Francisco main line. New York-to-Washington flights, which had operated regularly ever since Lieutenant George Boyle's wrong-way maiden voyage in May 1918, were halted on May 31, 1921; the feeder routes from Minneapolis and St. Louis to Chicago were abandoned a month later. With the elimination of these three routes, the new postal regime was able to economize by shutting down six airfields. Further saving came as the Post Office trimmed the airmail employee roster from 521 to 418, cut the pay of those who remained, and centralized its aircraft maintenance operations at Maywood, Illinois, near Chicago.

Perhaps even more important than these administrative rollbacks was a subtle and gradual change in the relationship between headquarters and the pilots. Pilots were now to be consulted about weather

he night airmail on the 22nd of March, 1924.

problems and deferred to in a way that represented a profound switch from Praeger's fly-or-else policy. Instead of flying whichever plane was available, pilots would now be assigned their own aircraft, and they might even have a say in the design if there were particular instruments or features they wanted. Moreover, their views would be considered on such subjects as night flying and the performance of their aircraft.

The change wrought early in the Harding administration boosted the morale of the pilots at the same time that it altered the character of air-mail headquarters in Washington. Now the service was less boastful and adventurous than it had been under the ebullient Praeger—but it was also more confident. Guided for the next half decade by capable and low-profile managers, the government's airmail enterprise would go quietly about the demanding task of developing transcontinental night-flying techniques that became a wonder of world aviation.

If the atmosphere at headquarters had become more tame and busi-nesslike, pilots still confronted plenty of gritty adventure in the day-to-day business of flying the mail, especially in the mountainous West. Indeed, pilot Paul Scott, who flew between Elko, Nevada, and Salt Lake City, experienced a spell in March of 1922 when trouble seemed to hound him every Friday. En route from Elko to Salt Lake on Friday, March 3, Scott was forced down on the Utah salt flats by a broken oil line. Trailed by a pack of wolves who remained a respectful 30 feet behind him, he hiked 27 miles to get help. On the following Friday a sudden blizzard compelled him to put down on the shore of the Great Salt Lake near sundown; this time he walked all night. On Friday the 17th, flying from Salt Lake to Elko, he landed at Elko in a high wind and careened into a plane parked on the field.

The most agonizing predicament that a mountain flier could get into was to find himself down and alone in the high-country winter, as Henry Boonstra found out for himself on the 9,400-foot-high summit of a Utah mountain in December 1922. Flying somewhat south of his usual course from Salt Lake City to Rock Springs, Boonstra belly-landed on Porcupine Ridge after his carburetor iced up in a snowstorm. The tricky mountaintop landing collapsed the plane's landing gear and damaged the fuselage but left him unhurt.

Boonstra moved off the windswept peak and down toward a ranch house he knew about in a valley several miles distant. Wading into waist-high snow, he used his suitcase as a prop as he tried to follow a stream bed down the mountainside. He swung the valise in front of him with each step and then pushed down on it to give himself leverage for the next difficult stride. His muscles ached as he stretched one leg and then the other out of the drifts. The snow continued to fall.

Boonstra struggled through the morning and afternoon and into the night, knowing that if he stopped for long to rest he might not be able to get started again. And then, soon after dawn the next morning, he broke out of the woods and saw a chimney that seemed to be only a couple of

A D.H.4 soars above the Rockies. At such heights the engine "has an odd sound, strangely clear in the rarefied air," recalled a journalist who flew the mail route in 1924. "It is here," he said, "that one's hand seeks the ring of the parachute instinctively—but perish the thought!"

miles away. It took him all that day to reach the ranch house. All told, he had spent some 33 painful and sleepless hours slogging nearly nine miles. "The muscles in my hips got so stiff that it took me weeks to get used to my legs again," he remembered.

The ranch that Boonstra eventually reached was occupied by a lone sheepherder who had no telephone. The man loaned the pilot a horse and guided him to the nearest village on the 18th, three days after he had dropped down on Porcupine Ridge. The airmail men at Salt Lake City and Rock Springs had meantime organized a widespread search employing both planes and ground parties, and a search plane had finally spotted his downed de Havilland.

True to the mail aviator's unwritten code of modesty, Boonstra professed astonishment at the fuss over his disappearance and denied that he had done anything special. The interest in his whereabouts, he said,

A D.H.4 clings to a snowbound bluff near Rock Springs, Wyoming, where pilot Robert Ellis landed it after being caught in a downdraft in January 1922. Ellis and the mail were pulled up to the plateau by a human chain of rescuers. In June the plane was dismantled and trucked out.

was a "revelation." In a congratulatory telegram to the search organizers, General Superintendent Carl Egge expressed the more prideful headquarters view: YOU NEED NOT TELL US THAT EVERY ONE OF THE BOYS VOLUNTEERED HIS SERVICES. WE KNOW IT. THAT SPIRIT IS RESPONSIBLE FOR THE SPLENDID RECORD MADE FOR THE SERVICE BY OUR BOYS. And that same spirit—the pilots' willingness to do their duty and more, whatever the conditions—would be summoned again for the next important challenge that the mail pilots faced.

Postal officials knew that the only way the Air Mail Service could really prove itself was to fly routinely at night. Only by voyaging through the dark on a regular schedule could the aerial postmen actually save money for bankers and businessmen—chiefly by speeding check clearances and accelerating fund transfers to save the daily interest charges on loans. But there were still many unanswered questions about the mechanics of a night flying operation: What kind of lights or beacons were needed, and how many? How far apart should they be? Should the planes be lighted as well? Could night flights over mountains— the hellish Alleghenies, for example—actually be considered? Jack Knight's nocturnal heroics had proved little beyond the fact that dogged determination and educated guesswork could sometimes pierce the void. What was needed for successful nighttime operations was a detailed plan that went well beyond a few bonfires to light the way.

Edward Shaughnessy, Otto Praeger's successor as head of the Air Mail Service, had preferred to postpone such a plan until more money was available. Then in early 1922 Shaughnessy was killed, one of 96 people who died when the roof of Washington's Knickerbocker Theater collapsed under more than two feet of snow. He was replaced by Paul Henderson, a Chicago businessman who also happened to be the son-in-law of one of the airmail's most persistent and powerful critics, Congressman Martin B. Madden of Illinois. Henderson's first impression was that airmail was "an impractical sort of fad," but he soon came to believe in it—and to feel that only through regular night flights could airborne mail justify itself. In the spring of 1922 he asked engineer Joseph V. Magee to study the problem and make recommendations.

Magee was not breaking entirely new ground—the French had experimented with beacons to guide night flights and the United States Army had laid out a 72-mile lighted airway between Columbus and Dayton, Ohio. But there was no regularly scheduled night flying anywhere in the world at the time.

Working diligently for more than a year, Magee came up with a plan calling for a system of beacons and emergency landing fields between Chicago and Cheyenne, the flatland heart of the transcontinental route. Terminals at Chicago, Iowa City, Omaha, North Platte and Cheyenne would be equipped with 36-inch revolving lights mounted on towers 50 feet high; the lights would sweep the horizon three times a minute with a

Hooked up to a truck, a crippled D.H.4 is ferried down a mountain road from its emergency landing site high in the Sierra in the mid-1920s. Even when mailplanes were smashed beyond repair, the Post Office had the wrecks hauled away in order to salvage valuable parts.

The faithful D.H.4

When the de Havilland D.H.4 joined the Air Mail Service in 1918, it was already famous as the best single-engined bomber of World War I. Designed in 1916 by the British aviation pioneer Sir Geoffrey de Havilland, the D.H.4 served with Britain's Royal Air Force in France, Belgium, Russia and the Near East. Almost 5,000 were built on license in the United States—the only American-made plane to see combat in the War.

In its civilian incarnation the completely overhauled D.H.4 proved a remarkably adaptable mailplane. In 1923 some D.H.4s were fitted with landing lights, underbelly flare boxes and lengthened exhaust pipes that shielded the pilot's vision from the engine's glowing exhaust: Thus modified, they became the first aircraft to regularly fly the mail at night.

The D.H.4 was powered by a 400-hp Liberty engine that gave it a top speed of 124 mph and a range of 250 miles. This is the refurbished model that was used by the Post Office for night flying.

beam visible in clear weather for more than 100 miles. At each of the emergency fields, which were roughly 25 miles apart, an 18-inch rotating beacon would blaze from atop a 50-foot tower. The course along the entire lighted airway would be marked at three-mile intervals by gaslights flashing 150 times per minute. This 902-mile illuminated aerial boulevard would be supplemented by floodlights at the airports, landing field boundary lights and powerful headlights mounted on the wings of the de Havillands. By April 1923 the beacon towers were rising, and the Postmaster General optimistically announced that night flying involved "scarcely more hazard than day flying."

The men who would deal directly with the hazard knew better. Dean Smith, who made his first nocturnal test flights at North Platte aided only by a bank of automobile headlights, found that night flying in good weather was simple enough, but that foul-weather problems, such as heavy clouds, precipitation or dense haze, were magnified in the dark, where it was harder to judge distance and height.

Most mail pilots were initially skeptical of the notion of regular night flights. "To say the least," Henderson reported, the aviators' reaction was "not encouraging." But their doubts seemed to fade as the details evolved. Polled by their two-and-a-half-year-old professional association, the Air Mail Pilots of America, on whether they believed in night flying for the Air Mail Service, 18 of 25 replied in mid-1923 with an unqualified yes; six others qualified their affirmative responses. Only E. Hamilton Lee said no. "I wanted to work in the daytime and have fun at night," he explained later. "How could you chase women when you worked nights?" The fun-loving Lee transferred to the New York-Cleveland sector, where flights took place in the daylight hours, though he would later join his fellow pilots in the night skies.

With all the beacons in place and a squadron of volunteer pilots ready to go, a full-dress rehearsal of round-the-clock operations was performed over four days in August 1923. Dean Smith flew the beacon-lit route between Chicago and Omaha on the first night and wrote later that it was "duck soup—the weather was perfect, the light of sunset lasted almost half the way and the harvest moon served as a floodlight." When he landed in Omaha at 11 p.m. "there must have been 100,000 people waiting—or so it seemed." Aside from a weather-caused delay to an eastbound flight in Wyoming, the eight transcontinental day-and-night trips went off without a hitch or a forced landing. The best west-to-east time was an impressive 26 hours and 14 minutes (in 11 relays), while the fastest performance between East and West, flown in 12 relays against the prevailing winds, was 29 hours and 38 minutes. Such service, if regularly maintained, could trim the normal transit time of coast-to-coast mail by nearly three days.

In their own businesslike way the men at headquarters were jubilant. The test had shown, Henderson declared, that night operations were "feasible and practical." Even so, the Post Office would have to switch off its beacons at the end of the August test and leave them off until the following summer: A dubious Congress had declined to appropriate enough money for further night flights.

With the development of successful night flying methods, the new postal administration's first few years had been crowned with a supreme technical achievement. But in human terms, the Air Mail Service's finest accomplishment during this period was a dramatic improvement in its safety record. In 1920, the fatalities per million miles flown had stood at 7.62; in 1921, the figure dropped to 3.66. In 1922, this key statistical gauge of operational safety declined to an impressive 0.57. Indeed, between July of 1921 and September of 1922 not a single pilot or other airmail employee died on duty, a record that won the service the National Aeronautic Association's coveted Collier Trophy for "the greatest achievement in aviation" in 1922.

The reason for the improvement was in part technological. A network of radio stations at the mail fields now permitted the continuous relay of weather data so that pilots had a better idea what to expect ahead. Parachutes, though still disdained as sissified by many pilots, were available by 1922. The quality of maintenance and repair work had also been improved. When a mailplane crashed now it was not because the pilot had been sent aloft in zero-visibility weather or consigned to the sky in a mysteriously flawed craft like the J.L. 6. The reasons were likely to be specific and unpredictable: a sudden ferocious wind like the one that caught the low-flying James "Dinty" Moore and slammed his plane onto a Wyoming hilltop, a defectively welded control stick that broke off in Howard C. Brown's hand over Ohio, the cutting of Clarence Gilbert's parachute cords on his plane's tail assembly as he tried to bail out in a blinding blizzard over Illinois.

When Moore and Brown were killed within three weeks of each other in December 1923, Postmaster General Harry New (Will Hays had departed the year before to become the movie industry's official censor)

A hacksaw, drill, vise, soldering iron, blowtorch and swivel-out workbench form the do-it-yourself emergency kit custom-built into pilot Randy Page's D.H.4. As head of the Maywood repair depot, Page applied his own flying experience to making improvements in the aircraft.

suspended all mail flights for four days so that mechanics could inspect every plane on the line. A few days later Paul Henderson stressed the new concern with safety when, in the words of an airman who was there, he told a group of pilots to "forget the airmail percentage. I would rather run at 25 per cent and not kill a man than run at 96 per cent and kill someone."

The Post Office demonstrated its concern for the pilots' well-being in countless large and small ways. The assignment of a single customized plane to each aviator was one example; another was a letter that Henderson sent to all mail pilots in early 1924. "Do not fly when you have any question about the condition of your ship," he told them. "Do not fly when you have any question as to the suitability of the weather." When in doubt, sit it out. Here was a change in traditional airmail policy so fundamental that a pilot could almost feel it with his fingertips.

The change in emphasis from delivery percentages to pilot safety was soon followed by an equally dramatic change in the airmail's operating area: The postal chiefs decided to venture into the aeronautically forbidding territory of Alaska. The proposal to fly the mail in Alaska came from Carl Ben Eielson, a broad-shouldered and somewhat scholarly North Dakota native who, like many mail pilots, had learned to fly during World War I. In 1922 he had migrated to Fairbanks, where he taught science and mathematics and coached the high school basketball team. Still smitten by aviation, Eielson acquired a Curtiss Jenny and supplemented his schoolteacher's pay by giving sightseeing rides and aerobatic shows. Late in 1923 he persuaded Washington to let him make periodic mail flights over the harshest and wildest country a postal pilot had ever looked down upon—the 280 miles of mountains and frozen wilderness between Fairbanks and McGrath. Regular air traffic of any kind was unknown in this vastness, and no flying had been attempted in the winter. Mail was normally delivered by dogsled, and it took 18 days each way.

The Post Office crated a de Havilland and shipped it to Eielson in early 1924. The idea was that he would make two one-day round trips a month on a contract basis. The Post Office viewed it as a short-term experiment; Eielson hoped it would evolve into a permanent business.

When he prepared to leave a Fairbanks ball field on his first trip, on February 21, 1924, the temperature was 5° below zero and Eielson was wearing a closetful of clothes—three pairs of heavy socks, long johns and two pairs of pants, a wool shirt and sweater, and a hooded reindeerskin parka. In addition to 164 pounds of mail, he carried a sleeping bag and 10 days' rations, but he knew that if he had a forced landing almost anywhere along this route the provisions would probably last longer than he would.

The skis that Eielson had attached to the landing gear struts dug down into three-foot-deep powdery snow as he gunned the engine and took off. When he was airborne he discovered that neither the air-speed indicator nor the compass worked, but he felt that he knew the terrain well enough to go ahead anyway. Flying a course over frozen rivers and broken valleys where roadhouses along the dogsled trail were 35 miles apart, he covered the distance in 2 hours and 50 minutes and landed on an iced-over river at 11:35 a.m. His only problem so far was that he had overdressed—he felt too warm.

At McGrath he ate lunch, collected 60 pounds of mail and refueled, but he ran into trouble when he tried to start the engine. No one in McGrath had ever seen an airplane before, much less helped start one, and Eielson had to crank the propeller himself and then scramble hastily into the cockpit. It was 2:35 p.m. by the time he got away. To reach Fairbanks by dusk he would have to fly a more direct—and more dangerous—course over unfamiliar territory.

He had gone about halfway on the return trip when the landmarks began to puzzle him. First, he saw a stream where no stream showed on his map. Then the settlement of Nenana, one of the few on the route, was not where it was supposed to be. Darkness descended as he hunted for the village. He began to think that he had mistaken one river for another. Clouds blotted out the stars. He was lost, Eielson finally realized, lost at night over the white Alaskan wilderness, armed with only a worthless compass, his memory and his instincts.

Feeling more desolate by the moment, Eielson droned through the Alaskan night for an hour with no notion of where he was. At last he saw a light and flew toward it. Guessing that it was a trapper's cabin, he decided to pass up the possibility of a warm bunk; the price of landing, he knew, would be a wrecked plane. He headed into the unknown once more. Returning to the mysterious river he had seen before, Eielson

Bundled against the cold, Carl Ben Eielson prepares to take off from Fairbanks on Alaska's maiden airmail flight, on February 21, 1924. Winging 280 miles to McGrath in three hours, Eielson outstripped the regular mail runs—carried out by dog teams like the one beside his D.H.4—by a full 17 days.

Second Assistant Postmaster General Paul Henderson (left) goes over the route for the first regularly scheduled night flight between Chicago and Cheyenne with Chicago's Maywood Field manager, O. D. Christner. The flight, with three stopovers, took place on July 1, 1924.

followed it until he spotted a flare flickering in the distance. "It turned out to be my home field," he wrote in a subsequent report to Henderson. "I guessed at the extremity of the field and went in." As he touched down he struck a tree and nosed over, but at least he was intact and among friends—the whole town had been waiting for him for more than an hour.

Eielson made seven more round trips to McGrath in the next few months, taking care to start back early enough to avoid a repeat of his unsettling debut. President Calvin Coolidge, who had taken office after Harding's death in 1923, heard about his adventures and dashed off a congratulatory note, but a crash landing on the eighth trip left Eielson's D.H.4 short of vital parts. By then, headquarters had lost interest in the Alaska venture and was busy with a higher-priority project—the long-deferred inauguration of regular all-night flights.

The Post Office was cleared to begin round-the-clock flights between the coasts when Congress allocated $2.75 million to the Air Mail Service for the fiscal year beginning July 1, 1924. Postal officials had spent much of the previous year, following the successful four-day test in August 1923, refining their facilities and extending the lighted airway to Rock Springs in the West and Cleveland in the East. The airmail publicity apparatus had clanked back into action as well, and an elaborate model of the transcontinental airway, 23 feet long, was set up in New York's Times Square in June; model planes, traversing the route on belts, passed through a red zone signifying daylight and a blue nighttime section pierced with pinholes of light representing beacons.

The spectacle of nocturnal takeoffs and landings—the sudden emergence of a single fleck of light from among the stars, while the great beacon punched holes in the night—restored the airmail's place in the public imagination to an eminence it had not enjoyed since Jack

Postal officials observing the trailbreaking Chicago-Cheyenne night flight gather in Omaha beside a D.H.4 equipped with landing lights. They are (from left) Central Division assistant superintendent Carlton Force, airmail chief Carl Egge, illumination engineer Joseph Magee and Central Division superintendent Duard B. Colyer.

Knight's daring flight. Large crowds turned out to watch the mailplanes take off in Chicago on opening night.

Despite a series of summer storms, the night mail performed with commendable precision during the first weeks of round-the-clock service. West-to-east airmail—aided by tail winds—regularly crossed the country in about 30 hours; the east-to-west journey averaged about 35 hours. The mail loads dropped sharply after the first few days of souvenir letters but then picked up again as bankers and businessmen began filling the special red-white-and-blue mailboxes that were placed at strategic locations in cities served by airmail.

The pilots, with only an occasional exception, seemed content with the new demands on their skill and nerve. It did not hurt that their mileage pay—from 5 cents to 7 cents a mile according to the terrain—was doubled at night. One of the exceptions was Randy Page. The Omaha field manager told a writer for the *National Geographic* that Page regularly swore "that each night flight would be his last. He'd run into a cloud or a patch of fog, lose sight of *every* light in the world, and then he'd hit a bump and the engine would sputter and backfire—

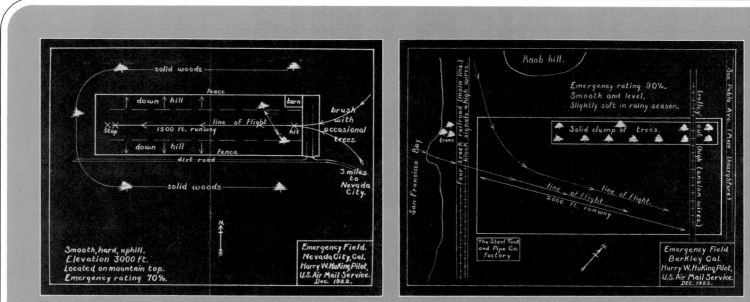

Hazards likely to be met at emergency fields—including "solid woods"—are charted on maps drawn by pilot Harry Huking in 1922.

Lighting the way for the night mail

"The Air Mail," wrote an admiring Army pilot, "is daily translating improbable facts into truths." Nothing could have been more improbable when the service began than a string of lights forming an aerial pathway from New Jersey to Utah. But this is what the Post Office managed to do by the mid-1920s, making night flying a reality.

Every 25 miles or so along the 2,045-mile route fields for emergency landings were built and outlined with lights. Then at each field a 50-foot steel windmill tower was erected and equipped with a revolving beacon that could be seen from the air for 60 to 70 miles on clear nights. And as an additional safety measure, smaller gas-burning beacons were placed at intervals between the emergency fields to guide the Air Mail Service pilots on their way.

everything inky black—it made his hair crawl around under his helmet, he said." Eventually, though, the Omaha beacon would swim into view and after landing Page would relent and agree to try it one more time.

Coast-to-coast trips were flown in seven relays; fresh pilots and planes took over in Cleveland, Chicago, Omaha, Cheyenne, Salt Lake City and Reno. The longest leg was the 476 nighttime miles from Omaha to Cheyenne; the shortest was the 184 miles across the Sierra from Reno to San Francisco. At fuel stops such as Iowa City and North Platte the ground crews scrambled into action as soon as the planes touched down. According to pilot Reuben Wagner, a plane would taxi in one end of a hangar open at both ends and a hose would descend from above to fill the fuel tank. Then the plane would taxi out the other side and roar down the runway. "The whole thing took about five minutes," Wagner recalled. "It was like a pit stop—I didn't even have to get out of the plane."

The boulevard of beacons was steadily improved as experience disclosed its weaknesses. More revolving lights were added until the distance between them averaged about 15 miles, while their size was increased from 18 inches to 24. By 1925, when the lighted airway

A beacon marks an emergency field near Omaha for a mailplane.

A shack houses the generator that powered this beacon.

A boundary light sits at the edge of an emergency field.

An engineer inspects a beacon with a photosensitive valve.

was extended to New York, it was one of the marvels of international aviation; no other country in the world had developed anything like it.

The workhorse de Havilland, refined by scores of improvements, was making an ever more impressive contribution in its own right. The quest for the perfect mailplane, which resumed with the beginning of night flying, had still failed to turn up an alternative to this hardy World War I veteran. Postal officials still bewailed the fact that the D.H.4 had not been designed with mail duty in mind, but they had tinkered with it so doggedly that they had made it their own. By one count the number of structural alterations amounted to more than 600.

To lower the plane's minimum speed and thus make night landings safer, aeronautical engineers designed new wings that reduced the landing speed from 60 to 45 miles per hour; but it also increased the maximum cruising speed (with a 500-pound load) by 10 miles an hour to 131. Airmail mechanics found that the gear connecting the Liberty engine's crankshaft with its camshaft would sometimes shear in flight, halting the engine and precipitating a hasty search for level ground. The solution was the installation of strong stub-toothed gears.

The Air Mail Service had mixed results in its experiments with various

E. Hamilton Lee, in flying togs, tests the microphone of an experimental plane-to-ground radiophone with a 200-mile range as postal officials stand by. Housed behind the pilot's seat in a D.H.4 (above) are the vacuum tubes of another radio, with a 100-mile range.

kinds of radio gadgetry. In one early attempt to follow a radio signal north from Washington to Philadelphia, pilot Kenneth McGregor flew above the clouds and dutifully obeyed a radioman's instructions until he ran out of fuel—on the outskirts of Norfolk, Virginia, 145 miles south of his starting place. Later attempts produced fitful successes followed by official declarations of optimism and then—silence. Jack Knight tested a 170-pound General Electric radio set with some success in 1923. With a receiver under his helmet and a transmitter on his chest, he relayed periodic reports on his position while flying from Omaha to North Platte at 2,000 feet; a 200-foot-long wire streaming behind the plane served as an antenna. But despite this and other promising tries the bulky radios never gained the Post Office's official blessing, and air-to-ground communication remained nothing more than a tantalizing possibility.

The pilots themselves came up with some ingenious navigational and flight instruments, though some dedicated seat-of-the-pants aviators agreed with the veteran Slim Lewis, who grumbled that an instrument panel was "just something to clutter up your cockpit and distract your attention from the railroad or river bed you're following." But most mail pilots recognized that reliable instruments, particularly turn-and-bank indicators that would enable them to fly blind in clouds or fog, could save their lives. Even a clock or watch could help a pilot who knew from experience exactly how long it took to cover a given distance; if the weather was foggy he could fly so many minutes and then nose down to the valley he remembered. And if the clock failed, native resourcefulness could sometimes produce an alternative timekeeping device, as pilot James D. Hill discovered on a fog-hounded trip from Bellefonte to New York. Entering the mist just east of Bellefonte, Hill recalled that he normally smoked one and a half cigars en route to Sunbury, in the Susquehanna valley. Glancing down every so often at the solid layer of fog beneath him, Hill puffed along at his regular pace, snuffed out his first stogie and lit another. When his second cigar was burned halfway down he dropped through the overcast and landed at Sunbury.

Pilots tried similarly imaginative techniques in search of ways to hold their planes level when they could not see the ground and use it as a point of reference. One taped a flat-backed, half-empty whiskey bottle to his instrument board and studied the level of the amber fluid therein; another tried a walnut tied to a string as a plumb bob. Several pilots experimented with a turn indicator used by military aviators, but they found that the air-intake tubes that activated it frequently became clogged with ice or mud. Wesley Smith, the most persistent tinkerer among the pilots, enlisted the aid of instrument specialist Howard Salisbury in developing a turn-and-bank device. First they mounted the turn indicator's air tubes on the exhaust pipes to eliminate the icing problem. Then they fashioned a bank indicator out of a curved six-inch-long glass tube with a steel ball inside it, on the principle of a carpenter's level.

With this device mounted in tandem with the turn indicator, the pilots had a crudely effective turn-and-bank instrument and greater confidence in their ability to fly through foul weather without losing their bearings. But though their touch with their new instruments improved with practice, few fliers went hunting for opportunities to use them. "For a long time the mental hazard was too great to allow us to stick our noses deliberately into blind weather," Dean Smith wrote later, "and our first productive use of the art usually came on some occasion when we inadvertently got caught in the stuff and had to fly our way out."

A lone airmail radio operator manning the Cheyenne radio shack listens through his headset to a report from another station. Responsible for receiving and transmitting flight and weather information, operators such as this one worked seven days a week.

By the summer of 1925 the United States airmail organization that had begun seven years earlier with a few Army pilots and a fleet of Curtiss Jennies was at the pinnacle of achievement. It operated a far-flung network of routes and fields and beacons and hangars and radio stations smoothly, efficiently and for the most part safely—there were only three deaths in 1924 and just one in 1925. American mail pilots had won a reputation for being among the most skilled and experienced cross-country aviators in the world. The lighted airway was a model that was studied by foreign aeronautical experts. One by one, the obstacles that had blocked the airmail's flight path—Congressional stubbornness, the fly-or-else policy, mountain barriers, mechanical weaknesses and the perils of the night—had been conquered.

The mail got through on time often enough to satisfy most of its customers, among them the financial institutions that were now reaping savings through the speed-up in collection times on checks and other financial instruments. The service was used by leading banks in nearly every major city, and one banker spoke for his colleagues nationwide when he said the airmail was of "inestimable value." Moreover, the service was promising to break even: The revenue for fiscal year 1925, while still short of expenses, was closer than it had ever been before.

The politicians had finally succumbed to the airmail's charms, and the public swarmed the terminals to watch night flights. Indeed, some citizens showed signs of giddiness on the subject of airmail. A San Francisco automobile dealer, for one, plastered himself with $718 in airmail stamps and tried to mail himself to New York as a parcel; the Post Office declined to accept the novel package. A Chicago woman asked about the possibility of airmailing her two children home from Colorado—she was told that mailplanes did not carry "perishable matter."

But there was a persistent irony in the government airmail's triumph, for the very dimensions of its success made its ultimate demise all but inevitable. Postal officials and congressmen had long maintained that the government had no interest in flying the mail indefinitely. As soon as the service could be operated profitably, they said, airmail routes would be put up for bids and turned over to private contractors. And the steady growth of American civil aviation had produced a number of entrepreneurs who were eager to carry the mail in their own planes.

Legislation authorizing the Postmaster General to contract with such companies or individuals had been introduced by Representative Clyde Kelly of Pennsylvania in 1922. The bill was defeated, but three years later its time had come. Supported by Henderson and other airmail leaders, the Kelly bill—entitled the Air Mail Act—was approved by Congress and signed by President Coolidge in February 1925. In July the Post Office advertised for bids on eight feeder routes running laterally to the transcontinental airway and connecting with such cities as Boston, Dallas and Los Angeles. The bids were to be opened in the fall.

Before it gradually faded away, however, the government mail line made one final conquest that may have been the sweetest of all—night

flights over the Hell Stretch between New York and Chicago. Bankers and businessmen had long wished for overnight flights linking the country's two largest financial centers, and Otto Praeger had promised such service nearly seven years earlier. But the Alleghenies had resisted all the way; emergency fields, in some sections only 10 miles apart, had to be slowly and laboriously cleared and lighted.

More than 15,000 people turned out at Hadley Field in New Jersey on the moonlit evening of July 1 to watch Dean Smith and J. D. Hill lift off on the initial after-dark trips to Cleveland. Congressman Fiorello H. La Guardia of New York, a longtime aviation booster, flew up from Washington in a Martin bomber for the occasion. Smith, the first of the two mail pilots to go aloft, returned immediately to the field with engine problems but shortly took off again and negotiated the first leg to Bellefonte with no difficulty. Then engine failure forced him down near Kylertown, Pennsylvania. After he had waited two hours a new plane arrived from Cleveland. Smith took off and immediately encountered a head wind. He ran out of fuel near Solon, Ohio, released a parachute flare and saw that there was no place to land. "I came in over the trees," he recalled, "dismal at having to wreck the ship and on such an important flight." The plane cartwheeled and turned over, but Smith walked away unhurt and roused a farmer to help him retrieve the mail. Gazing at the twisted and upside-down de Havilland, the farmer asked: "Do you always land this way?"

The cigar-chewing Hill had better luck than Smith did. He flew without incident to Cleveland, where there were still some stragglers on hand from a throng of more than 200,000 spectators who had shown up at the new municipal airport to greet pilot Shirley Short when he flew in from Chicago some time earlier. A woman spectator had been so moved by Short's flight that she composed an instant ode entitled "Hail, Brave Messenger of the Air." Another large crowd had gathered at Chicago, where an enthusiastic *Tribune* reporter succumbed to a temptation to rhapsodize about the planes' postal cargo—"romance and finance, the sad tidings of sickness and perhaps the glad news of births."

The truly glad news for the Air Mail Service was that the first three months of night runs over the Hell Stretch fully justified both public enthusiasm and official confidence. Business was lively, revenues exceeded costs, the crowds flocked to see the nightly show and mishaps were surprisingly rare. The Post Office reported that 100 per cent of the miles scheduled to be flown in August were in fact flown. Many concluded that the Alleghenies had at last been tamed. They were wrong.

Mustachioed, courtly Charlie Ames gunned his engine on the Hadley Field runway a few minutes before 10 p.m. on October 1, 1925, and took off into an overcast with a 5,000-foot ceiling. As he headed west over Bethlehem and Allentown, Pennsylvania, en route to his first stop at Bellefonte, the ceiling lowered, but visibility remained fair. Bellefonte was reporting a 1,500-foot ceiling with visibility at 15 miles. This was not good, but Ames had flown in worse conditions. A former Army flight instructor and barnstormer, the 31-year-old Ames had been flying the mail on the Hell Stretch off and on since 1920. A forced landing in 1922 had left him with a permanently stiff leg, the result of a break at the knee. As he droned past the first ramparts of the Alleghenies the thick clouds were settling over the hills and blotting out the shadowy landmarks. He had enough fuel for about four and a half hours in the air, which would almost get him to Cleveland. He was due at Bellefonte at 11:30.

Bellefonte field clerk Charlie Gates, who had spent the day on jury duty, went to the airport that night to see if the planes were getting through the worsening weather. The Cleveland-Bellefonte flight had been scrubbed, as had a scheduled second section out of Hadley. Ames was flying the only plane due in. By now the clouds were below the peaks on Nittany Mountain, to the east of the field. Gates started calling the emergency fields east of Bellefonte to see if the caretakers had spotted Ames. Sunbury, 50 miles away on the Susquehanna, reported that he had passed. The man at 30-mile-distant Hartleton said Ames had been by there, too. The caretaker at Woodward, only 22 miles from Bellefonte, said he had heard the plane but could not see it. Gates and the other crewmen spread out over the mist-draped field and listened for Ames's engine.

By 3 a.m. it was obvious that the long-overdue pilot was down somewhere—his fuel was gone by now—but where? He had not called either Hadley or Cleveland to report a forced landing. The Bellefonte workers telephoned farmers who lived near the route, but no one had heard a crash. As the foggy morning dawned, a group began to scour the thickly forested hills that bracketed a succession of valleys east of town. Two planes stood by to help, but the weather grounded them.

Wearing bulky parachutes, Charles Ames (right) and Wesley Smith compare notes at New Jersey's Hadley Field. Several months later Ames, an experienced bad-weather pilot, crashed into a fog-cloaked Allegheny ridge while flying the mail at night between Hadley and Cleveland.

The locals knew that if Ames lay injured somewhere in this sprawling and intimidating wilderness it could take days to find him. He did have a revolver—which might gain attention and maybe even a meal—and some chocolate. But even an aerial search, as the Bellefonte newspaper pointed out, could not "spy into the thousands of mountain ravines" where his plane might be "hidden from sight by the leaves." At the end of the first day Ames was officially listed as missing.

The first lead turned up the next day, a Saturday. Two farmers who lived near Clarion, 112 miles northwest of Bellefonte, said that they had seen a plane between midnight and 1 a.m. during the night Ames disappeared. Three other people who lived in that area claimed to have heard an engine at about the same time. It was possible that Ames had decided to overshoot socked-in Bellefonte and fly on in hopes of out-running the weather. If so, the area to be searched was now more than 100 miles long. Planes and ground parties scoured the Clarion region through the weekend and into the following week without success.

On Monday, October 5, the story of the missing pilot was on the front page of *The New York Times*. Reporters converged on Clarion and Bellefonte much as they had descended on the Kentucky cave country earlier that year to cover the saga of cave explorer Floyd Collins, who was trapped in a narrow underground shaft. The mystery of Ames's whereabouts was the main journalistic attraction, but airmail accidents were rare enough now to be newsworthy in themselves; the last fatality had occurred nearly 10 months before. Rain still hampered the search—"the worst flying weather in the history of the Air Mail Service," a Post Office newsletter called it—but more planes and pilots continued to arrive to take part. Superintendent Carl Egge arrived on the scene to direct the operations. He speculated that Ames might still be alive but somehow trapped or incapacitated.

Three days passed with no sign of Ames or his plane. Pennsylvania National Guardsmen and 1,000 students from Pennsylvania State College joined the search. Reporters kept the local Western Union operators working overtime by unearthing more self-proclaimed eyewitnesses—among them two raccoon hunters and a pair of railroad workers. The Post Office offered a $500 reward. Army aviators, along with Ames's brother mail pilots, were summoned to help: Hamilton Lee came from Chicago, Dean Smith returned from a hunting vacation in Nova Scotia. Meanwhile, a vicious rumor had begun to circulate that Ames had absconded to Canada with a bundle of air-mailed securities.

A team of searchers found Ames and his plane on Nittany Mountain on Sunday, October 11, ten days after he disappeared. The pilot had died almost instantly of a fractured skull when his plane smacked into the mountainside about 200 feet below the summit, shearing branches off trees and smashing into a large rock. The autumn-hued oaks and dense underbrush had concealed the wreckage so effectively that earlier searchers had come within a few hundred feet of the plane without seeing it. The position of Ames's feet, still wrapped casually around the control stick, indicated that he had not realized he was in danger. Investigators surmised that Ames must have thought he was several hundred feet higher than he was because his altimeter had not allowed for the difference in barometric pressure between New Jersey and Bellefonte. Instrument man Howard Salisbury promptly set about devising an altimeter with a built-in barometric correction—too late for Charlie Ames, but not for those who came after him.

With the decision to phase gradually into an all-contract operation—an air transport service owned by the Ford Motor Company began mail flights from Detroit to Chicago and Cleveland in February 1926—the pioneering days of the government airmail were over. Post Office pilots continued to dare the mountains, the weather and the night on the transcontinental route until the summer of 1927, while contract lines initiated service to St. Louis, Boston and other cities. The long search for a successor to the de Havilland ended in 1926 with the appearance of

After Charles Ames's D.H.4 disappeared near Bellefonte, the Post Office handed out thousands of posters announcing a reward (inset) for anyone finding the lost pilot. A 15-year-old boy finally discovered Ames's body in the wrecked fuselage a quarter mile below the Hecla Gap beacon light.

REWARD
$500

To the Person or Persons who FIND Pilot in Mail Plane Lost Thursday Night or Friday Morning.

NOTIFY   Air Mail Field, Clarion, Pa.

the Douglas M-series mailplanes, which could carry nearly twice the load and travel farther and faster on a tank of fuel. Dean Smith and Earl Ward flew the last government mailplanes into New York on August 31, 1927, and a few weeks later the magazine *Aviation* said in a valedictory salute that "the United States air mail endeared itself to all who gave their best efforts to the development of aviation."

It endeared itself especially to those who served it best, the pilots who would now fan out to find employment with the private contractors. "I loved what I did, loved flying," Hamilton Lee would recall more than half a century afterward. "We could fly at any altitude, fly under bridges, drop a newspaper to our friends if we wanted to. Today they sit up there at 35,000 feet. What fun can they have? Oh, those were great days. They were dangerous days too, but you didn't mind that—that was nice in a way, too. If it wasn't for that memory I'd go nuts. I live on it. I still think about it when I go to sleep at night." ～

Treasures of the airmail

Among the most vivid reminders of the early days of airmail are the stamps, envelopes and postcards associated with many of the airmail's stellar achievements—and with some of the not so great moments as well.

The most valuable American stamp, the so-called inverted Jenny *(right),* was the product of a printer's error. In the Post Office Department's haste to issue a commemorative stamp before the first flight of the United States Air Mail Service on May 15, 1918, an overworked pressman took sheets of partially completed stamps and, without looking, ran them through his press. Several hundred 24-cent stamps were thus imprinted with a perfect representation of the first Curtiss Jenny to fly the mail, except that the aircraft was flying upside down.

Embarrassed Post Office officials managed to find and destroy all the sheets but one—it had been bought by an avid collector. Realizing the rarity of his prize, he refused to relinquish it and instead sold the sheet for $15,000.

As nations around the world began to fly the mail, each took to issuing its own special airmail stamps and these constitute a chronicle of aviation in themselves. But it is airmail postcards and envelopes, such as those on pages 104-105, that best convey the excitement—and at times the danger—associated with flying the mail. They also reveal the pride people took in the accomplishment: The Jenny stamp on the envelope below was initialed by six postal officials (including Otto Praeger, the Second Assistant Postmaster General), all of whom had a hand in making the first American airmail possible.

The inverted Jenny—whose central motif was printed
upside down—belonged to a sheet of 100 stamps that sold for
$24 in 1918. In 1982 the estimated value of a block
consisting of four such stamps was $610,000.

Autographed by President Woodrow Wilson before the
United States Air Mail Service's first official flight, this historic
envelope was sold at auction for $1,000 to support the wartime
relief efforts of the American Red Cross.

AUSTRIA

DANZIG

FRANCE

BELGIAN CONGO

DENMARK

EGYPT

LITHUANIA

COSTA RICA

GERMANY

BOLIVIA

SWEDEN

UNITED STATES

NICARAGUA

RUMANIA

ICELAND

HONDURAS

CHILE

SWITZERLAND

BRAZIL

GREECE

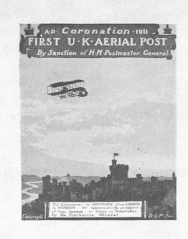

To celebrate George V's coronation, this envelope bearing an artist's rendering of Windsor Castle was issued in 1911 for mail flights between London and Windsor.

A souvenir of the world's first official airmail flight, a 1911 postcard bears an Allahabad, India, postmark.

This Japanese postcard, designed for a 1919 airmail flight contest between Tokyo and Osaka, depicts the evolution of Japan's postal service.

A 1918 Austrian envelope recalls the world's first international airmail—a wartime route between Austria and occupied Russia.

On this envelope, a well-known aviation writer scrawled a congratulatory note to the head of the United States Air Mail Service.

The world's first airmail stamp—a special delivery stamp overprinted with an airmail designation—appears on a 1917 envelope from Italy.

This envelope was postmarked on the first day of round-the-clock airmail service between New York and San Francisco.

The plane carrying this letter crashed into a tree. Only 75 of a total 800 pounds of mail were rescued from the burning aircraft.

Evincing the camaraderie that typified pilots of Aéropostale, France's enterprising airmail line, Antoine de Saint-Exupéry (left) and Henri Guillaumet clasp

...shoulders beneath a Laté 28 in South America in 1930.

4
European trailblazers

The prosperous-looking, bespectacled young man who strode so purposefully from one government office to another during the Parisian summer of 1918 was clearly no crackpot. At 35, Pierre Latécoère was a man of substance and accomplishment. An industrialist in the city of Toulouse in southern France, Latécoère, combining his patriotism and his drive for profit, had converted his railway-coach factory during the war with Germany into one of the country's largest producers of warplanes. Sober and shrewd, self-assured if perhaps a bit cold, Latécoère was a businessman who kept his eyes and his mind open.

But the bureaucrats hardly knew what to make of his proposal to establish a postal airline that would carry mail from France to Spain and French Morocco and then down the bulge of the North African coast to Dakar—some 2,900 miles—in two and a half days. And that was only the beginning. Dakar was to be the jumping-off place for transatlantic flights that would connect with a network of air routes on the east coast of South America. Ultimately, a letter written by a Bordeaux wine merchant or a Marseilles importer would reach Rio de Janeiro in a week or Buenos Aires a day later; by conventional shipborne mail such a communication would take more than three weeks.

Latécoère's audacious vision becomes even more breathtaking when viewed in the aeronautical context of that Armistice year of 1918: Most aircraft of the time, such as the Curtiss Jennies employed by the just-inaugurated United States Air Mail Service and the de Havillands that would soon replace them, had a range of no more than 250 miles on a tank of fuel. The few mail routes that had been attempted before this time, in France, Germany, Austria and Italy as well as the United States, had traversed settled and hospitable country where friendly farmhouses and railroad lines, those most dependable of navigation aids, were never far away.

By contrast, a mail route along the North African coast would cross one of the planet's emptiest and least forgiving barrens, the Sahara, an expanse roamed by nomadic peoples of several tribes that were known generally to Europeans of the time as Moors. The Moors were devout Muslims who deeply resented the foreign occupation of their lands, and they were frequently hostile toward the intruders. Airfields, except in a few widely separated cities, were nonexistent. Yet Latécoère, with little knowledge of aviation, envisioned an eventual three-continent air link-up—and this at a time when the first aerial conquest of the Atlantic was still a year away. Surprised that a man of such proven practicality would espouse such a preposterous idea—and at such a time, with the War still going on—the government officials Latécoère visited were coolly polite but noncommittal.

It was primarily the boldness of Latécoère's vision that distinguished his scheme from the ideas of his air-minded contemporaries in other European countries. The War had furnished a showcase that demonstrated the airplane's capabilities, and even before the Armistice a few irregular and short-term mail routes, mainly limited to military functions, had fluttered into life. The British had flown Army correspondence across the Channel to Belgium as early as 1915; Italy operated a route between Rome and Turin for a while in 1917, and the Germans flew mail between Berlin and Cologne for four months in early 1918. But the most ambitious of the wartime routes was a 700-mile-long military line between Vienna and Kiev in the then-independent Ukraine.

The main reason for the Austria-Ukraine route was hunger: The Ukraine had the food that the starving Austrians desperately needed. Telegraph lines and railroads had been disrupted by war and revolution, so an air service seemed to be the best means of establishing rapid communications with Ukrainian food suppliers.

The officer in command of the mail line, Colonel August Raft von Marwil, made a reconnaissance flight in March 1918 in a Brandenburg biplane with a single 200-horsepower engine. Arriving in Kiev after three days of short hops and meetings with ground-support crews along the way, the colonel and his observation officer soon discovered that they had indeed flown to a land of plenty. A long table in their hotel dining room was piled high with meat, fish, breads, vegetables and several varieties of caviar. "All this was eaten standing up," the colonel reported, "without forgetting to wash down every new course with a glass of water-clear vodka." Taking with him some 11 pounds of caviar and the memory of a gloriously self-indulgent evening, Raft von Marwil flew the return trip to Vienna in a single day, logging 10 hours in the air and stopping four times for fuel.

The line that was inaugurated soon afterward carried military and private mail, along with an occasional passenger, for seven months. It operated under several disadvantages, including primitive weather forecasting, shaky ground communications, inaccurate maps and a shortage of good planes and pilots, many of whom were still needed for full-time combat duty. Nevertheless, the Vienna-to-Kiev run functioned with no fatalities and only a few forced landings. After one such emergency, a pilot reported that he had set his craft down in a Ukrainian wheat field so bountiful that the stalks were higher than the plane; when the flier returned from making a telephone call, he said, it took a platoon of soldiers to find his plane.

Trouble of a different sort arrived when Hungary, the other half of the Austro-Hungarian Empire, insisted on having its own airmail service.

Launching the world's first international airmail service, two Austrian Army fliers take off from Vienna for Kiev in a Brandenburg biplane on March 20, 1918. Commanded by August Raft von Marwil (inset), the flights expedited starving Austria's trade with Russia's food-rich Ukraine.

Raft von Marwil, grumbling about the additional demands on his men and aircraft, opened a Vienna-Budapest route on July 4. Nine days later his chief Hungarian pilot and a crewman were killed when their biplane suddenly and mysteriously exploded on a flight to Vienna; many suspected sabotage. Before the month was out two more airmen perished when their plane crashed shortly after takeoff from Budapest. Again, there were rumors of sabotage. The Minister of War promptly closed down the Vienna-Budapest line, although the Vienna-Kiev route continued to operate until the final dissolution of the Austro-Hungarian Empire a few months later.

Pierre Latécoère, meanwhile, had been undeterred by Paris' unenthusiastic reaction to his projected France-to-South America mail route, and waited only a few weeks after the Armistice of November 11, 1918, before moving the first piece of his ambitious mosaic into place. On Christmas morning he rode as a passenger in one of his own single-engined Salmson biplanes on a trailblazing journey from Toulouse to Barcelona, Spain. Skirting the high peaks of the Pyrenees, Latécoère and his pilot crossed the Spanish frontier and landed safely in Barcelona that afternoon. On his return to Toulouse he added extra fuel tanks to another Salmson and dispatched his deputy, an aristocratic and much-decorated former French military flier named Beppo de Massimi, to discuss overflight rights and landing sites with the Spanish government.

The Italian-born Massimi brought to the enterprise a formidable endowment of personal charm and diplomatic skill, traits that comple-

In fur-trimmed coat and felt hat, Toulouse aircraft manufacturer Pierre Latécoère arrives by chauffeured auto at the Montaudran airfield on Christmas Day, 1918. Behind him waits the Salmson biplane that will carry him aloft on the inaugural flight of his newly founded airline.

mented Latécoère's shrewdness and vision. In addition, as an airman himself, Massimi was in a position to recruit the most talented of his wartime comrades. He scored his first triumph for Latécoère by persuading the Spaniards, over the objections of the powerful German colony in Madrid, to permit French planes to fly along the Spanish coast and land in Spanish cities. His second and even greater achievement was his recruitment of Didier Daurat, his wartime squadron commander, as a pilot. Tough and demanding, a gifted leader who was obsessed with the mission of the airmail, Daurat would in time become the heart and soul of the Latécoère Line in a way that far exceeded the similar role of Otto Praeger in the early years of the United States Air Mail Service.

With the Spanish mollified, the next step was to check their landing fields. In February 1919 Latécoère boarded one Salmson while Massimi climbed into another for a tandem test flight down the coast to Barcelona and Alicante. Massimi's plane, flown by a pilot named Lemaître, landed and refueled at Barcelona and flew on to Alicante, where the airmen were surprised to see a crowd assembled around an astoundingly tiny landing strip. It turned out that the Spanish had misunderstood their request for a 2,000-foot-long runway and had instead cleared a landing strip of 2,000 square feet—about the size of a tennis court. Predictably, Massimi's plane overran this miniature runway and bumped through an adjoining field of stones. Massimi, his nose bleeding, waited out a ceremonial welcome and then set the crowd to clearing a larger area for Latécoère's anticipated arrival.

But Latécoère, who was piloting himself, had meanwhile overshot Barcelona, landed on a beach near Tortosa and spent several hours scrounging for fuel. When he finally reached Alicante he missed the cleared field and slammed into the rocks. Emerging from his plane with a sore forehead, he pronounced himself otherwise satisfied and ready to move on to Morocco.

Two weeks later he did exactly that, this time prudently yielding the controls to Lemaître. On arriving in the capital city of Rabat, the canny Latécoère shucked his leather aviator's jacket, donned a straw hat and grabbed a bouquet of French violets he had brought as a gift for the wife of the French governor of Morocco. He had also brought along a sack of French mail. The governor, unable to resist this adroit blend of technology and chivalry, approved Latécoère's request to land his mailplanes in Morocco. Latécoère promptly returned to Paris, where he finally managed to get the government's blessing, along with the promise of a subsidy and war-surplus aircraft. Lignes Aériennes Latécoère—the Line, as it would come to be called—was officially in business.

A shortage of planes during the next few months limited the company's operations to the Toulouse-Barcelona run, but the government made good on its promise in late summer: Fifteen single-engined Breguet observation planes were turned over to Latécoère. Stronger and hardier than the Salmsons and equipped with 300-horsepower Renault engines, the Breguets became the French equivalent of the de Havillands of the United States Air Mail Service—the sturdy workhorses of the postal fleet.

The arrival of the Breguets enabled Latécoère to dispatch Didier Daurat to Casablanca on September 1 on the first regularly scheduled France-to-Morocco mail flight, with refueling stops at Barcelona, Alicante, Malaga and Tangier. Weekly at first, the one-day trips to North Africa were soon increased to twice and then to three times a week, until finally they were flown daily.

The French pilots quickly learned, as American aviators were finding at about the same time, that negotiating a mountain route in November and December was a different proposition from flying that course in September. On the line south from Toulouse the winter enemies were sudden blizzards that blocked the passes through the Pyrenees, precipitous vertical air currents, dark mists that formed along the coast, and violent winds out of the north, some of them fierce enough to drive a plane backward. Aviator Jean Rodier and mechanic François Marty-Mahé disappeared in the Mediterranean near the mountainous frontier between France and Spain in 1920; two more men died soon afterward when their plane crashed into a rocky Spanish hillside in a storm.

Latécoère's mechanics studied the lessons of every mishap: When torrential rains ripped pieces off the wooden propellers, they added metal plates to reinforce them; when the Breguets' weak braces and rods gave way they were rebuilt and strengthened. And both pilots and ground crews learned that in some ways a daily all-weather schedule demanded even more of men and equipment than did wartime flying.

As Latécoère's newly selected director of operations, Daurat was busily weeding out the more fainthearted pilots, those who preferred their hotel rooms in Toulouse or a café in Tangier to flying through storms, and establishing a rigorous pilot-training program that emphasized an intimate knowledge of engines. The fliers were taught to dismantle and rebuild the Renault engines on which their lives—and the mail—depended. Daurat saw his mission as the creation of a disciplined and dedicated corps of fliers, a cadre whose first loyalty was to the Line. The French writer Joseph Kessel, assessing Daurat's achievements, summed up the director's approach to his pilots: "Leave them to their nature and nothing good will come of it. Give them a collective goal; place this goal, by the unreasonableness that you show, at an almost inaccessible height, in a competition, a rivalry without end, and you make out of the soft human clay a substance of quality."

Daurat ran a harsh and demanding flight school, and not every airman passed. On one occasion a freshly hired aviator was scheduled to make his first flight from Toulouse to Barcelona on a day when fog hugged the Pyrenees. An older pilot volunteered to make the run in his place because of the weather, but Daurat insisted that the beginner fly because he needed the experience. The young pilot lost his way and died when he flew into a mountainside.

The number of letters borne annually by the Toulouse-Casablanca line increased from 9,124 in 1919 to 1,407,352 in 1922, and the volume of mail doubled in the 12 months that followed. But the Line had its problems as well. An attempt to inaugurate a new route between Casablanca and Oran, Algeria, had to be abandoned after two months because of the hazards posed by the Atlas Mountains. A pilot died at Barcelona, two died at Gibraltar and another perished at Alicante; an airman and two passengers were killed near Granada in southern Spain. Even so, Latécoère had decided it was time to expand: The Line would now take on the vast Sahara.

The 1,700 miles between Casablanca and Dakar would be the proving ground for Latécoère's dream of linking Europe and South America. If he could conquer the mechanical, logistical, political and physical obstacles presented by the Sahara, the dream would be a long step closer to fulfillment. The first leg of the route, the 260 miles from Casablanca to Agadir, Morocco, crossed country that was largely settled. But beyond Agadir lay a void—hundreds of miles of undulating dunes and searing desert unbroken by tree or bush. The planes would of course hug the Atlantic shoreline, where—in the Spanish Sahara—a few isolated forts perched on the edge of the desert like stone-turreted mirages. The Spanish authorities would have to be cajoled once again, this time to permit the French to establish airdromes in Spain's African colony.

From Agadir the Line would jump 300 miles to Cape Juby, the site of a lonely Spanish fort, and then 380 miles more to another fort at Villa Cisneros. From there it was 235 miles farther to Port-Étienne, the next oasis, and then another 385-mile leap to St.-Louis, Senegal. Dakar, the jumping-off point for Latécoère's projected South American venture, lay 140 miles farther down the coast. Bands of armed and inhospitable Moors roamed the sands between these outposts, menacing their European overlords at every opportunity. A downed pilot was fair game, and like everything else in this blazing waste he was valuable only insofar as he could help the Moors survive; holding him for ransom was the obvious way to make money out of him.

In May 1923 three Breguets set out in convoy to chart the course to Dakar. All three put down at the end of the first day at Juby, where the Spanish commander briefed the crews on the ruinous humidity and the nightly raids of the local Moors. On the second day one plane made it through to Dakar while the other two struggled into Port-Étienne after surviving various mechanical problems. By the third day they were all in Dakar, but one plane had to be abandoned when it broke down on the return trip and could not be repaired.

Proving that his planes could reach Dakar, however haphazardly, was only part of the task confronting Latécoère in the desert. The Spanish governors of Río de Oro had to be placated. Fields and hangars (to protect the planes from both humidity and Moors), fuel depots and radio stations had to be erected at the landing sites. The Line would also need kidnap insurance: Some 30 long-robed representatives of various Saharan tribes were summoned to a meeting and given money in exchange for their promise to guarantee the safety of downed pilots and their planes. All of this took time, and regular flights to Dakar could not begin until mid-1925.

In the meantime the restless Latécoère sent an emissary to South America to open talks with the governments of Brazil, Uruguay and Argentina about establishing mail lines there. He also made several attempts to inaugurate a route across the Mediterranean to Algeria, experimenting with both the lumbering Lioré et Olivier seaplane and a trimotor Caudron landplane before settling on the seaplane and beginning flights between Alicante and Oran in early 1924. Their radio equipment was still somewhat primitive, so the pilots brought carrier pigeons along for the inevitable emergencies.

At the same time, the spirit of competition and perfectionism that Daurat was trying to establish had begun to take hold, elevating mail flying into a kind of religion. André Dubourdieu, one of the young pilots recruited in 1924 and 1925, was thrilled when he was ordered to fly one of the final test flights to Dakar. Bursting with pride at "being charged with such a grand excursion at only 24," he ascended from Toulouse with three other pilots in late April, 1925, "loaded down like Arab donkeys" with spare parts and enough fuel for seven hours in the air.

After a stop at Alicante, Dubourdieu crossed the Strait of Gibraltar and cruised placidly along the Moroccan coast until he neared Agadir;

Close by the French compound at Africa's Cape Juby, three
Breguet biplanes sit ready to fly mail relays for the
Latécoère Line. In this "vast sandy void," as Antoine de Saint-
Exupéry described it, all that stood between the French airmen
and hostile nomads was a barbed-wire fence.

then his laboring engine failed and sent him into a dead-stick glide toward the sand. The plane's landing gear dug into the desert and caught, tipping the craft up on its nose. His companions flew on to Agadir while Dubourdieu commandeered a horse and made his way to the nearest town. A few days later a new plane arrived from Casablanca and Dubourdieu and two of the other French pilots took off for Cape Juby. The fourth stayed behind to set up a permanent base in Agadir.

Arriving at Juby, Dubourdieu found that the Spanish were still touchy about their jurisdiction; he and his mechanic were denied permission to remain there as the nucleus of a permanent detachment. At Port-Étienne, the next stop, they had to remove their plane's defective engine and replace it with a new one recently arrived from France. Dubourdieu and the two remaining pilots decided to stir up a little excitement on their approach to St.-Louis, Senegal, by buzzing the town in wing tip-to-wing tip formation, but their plan went awry when one of them impatiently flew ahead and another was delayed by an overheated engine; they limped in one at a time. Twenty days later the first regular airmail followed them into Dakar, and another piece of the Latécoère mosaic was in place.

It was less than two months after the opening of the Dakar route when aviators and Moors clashed for the first time. Two pilots, one named Ville and the other Rozès, were flying within sight of each other when the engine of Rozès's plane suddenly cut out. Moments after he brought his plane down on a beach, a group of Moors materialized from behind a dune—"what they live on nobody seems to have discovered," a British journal commented—and opened fire on the plane with rifles just as Ville landed to assist his downed companion. Ville squeezed off several rounds from his pistol, killing one Moor and driving the rest back. Rozès scrambled out of his crippled plane and climbed in behind Ville, who hurriedly took off amid a fresh fusillade of Moorish gunfire.

Aviators of the Line had another close call several weeks later after a pilot named Léopold Gourp spotted four fishermen waving near their grounded boat on a desolate stretch of beach. A few miles away he saw a band of Moors headed toward the stranded men. When Gourp reported the incident in Dakar two rescue planes flew immediately to the scene, and again an escape was accomplished with only minutes to spare. Next it was the youthful Dubourdieu's turn. Flying alone and forced down by the hard desert wind called the simoom, he was taken captive by Moors and released only after a ransom was paid.

The Casablanca-based pilots finally informed Daurat that they would no longer fly the desert route to Dakar. Daurat compromised by ordering that all flights over Río de Oro be flown in convoys of two or three planes. He also assigned friendly Arab interpreters to ride with the pilots so that they could negotiate their release if trouble developed. When the impetuous Marcel Reine crash-landed amid rocks and cactus south of Agadir in December, it was his interpreter who saved his life—at a price of 4,500 francs. The interpreters, many of whom had never seen an

The most celebrated pilot of the Latécoère Line, Jean Mermoz, recuperates after his three-day captivity by the Moors in May of 1926. Forced down with engine trouble in the Mauritanian desert, he was held by a band of veiled warriors until they received a ransom of 1,000 pesetas.

aircraft before the mailplanes arrived, made an easy adjustment to this marvel of the modern world. They seemed to take to flying naturally, a British periodical reported, curling up in the mail compartments and slumbering peacefully between crises.

In the spring of 1926 another pilot was taken prisoner and ransomed, but for this man, Jean Mermoz, it was merely the first in a career of adventures that would make him one of the most celebrated aviators of his time. The handsome, dashing and athletic Mermoz had a genius for the bravura gesture and a yen for the spotlight; every Latécoère pilot knew the story of his first flight test in front of Didier Daurat. Mermoz had looped the plane, made a series of steep turns and then sideslipped to a delicate landing. "We want pilots here, not acrobats," a fuming Daurat told him and sent him back to the workshop for a spell before letting him fly again. When Mermoz came down in the desert, he was bound hand and foot and placed in a cage atop a camel, where he bumped along painfully for three days before a black-veiled Arab chief agreed to accept a ransom for him.

A couple of other pilots were not so fortunate. While they were flying in convoy, one of them, Léopold Gourp, was forced down by engine failure on the bleak Río de Oro coast in November 1926. His colleague Henri Erable, accompanied by a Moorish interpreter and a Spanish mechanic, landed to assist Gourp, but when he came down he broke a propeller and punctured a tire; now both planes were disabled. Before long a band of Moors appeared, led by an Arab who had developed a hatred of the French while serving with the French Army in North Africa. The Moors opened fire immediately, killing Erable and the mechanic outright and gravely wounding Gourp in the leg. Gourp was loaded atop a camel, where his suffering became so acute that he eventually tried to commit suicide by swallowing iodine. His captors then left him

Outside their rude barracks, pilots and mechanics of the Line laugh at a colleague's antics. Pulling on the ear of the man at right is their pet ape Kiki.

for dead in the sand. The interpreter was released and reached Cape Juby in time to direct a rescue party, which found Gourp and took him to a hospital in Casablanca. Ten days later he died, not from his wound but from the poison.

Back in Toulouse, meanwhile, Daurat confronted his newest recruit, a tall and broad-shouldered young man whose protruding eyes gave him a look of perpetual surprise. Antoine de Saint-Exupéry, born in 1900 into an aristocratic provincial family that had fallen on difficult times, had developed a passion for flying during his service with the French air force following World War I. When he turned up in Daurat's office at the age of 26 he had only recently settled on flying as a career, after several false starts in other directions. A capable and courageous—if sometimes preoccupied—pilot, he would later find his true vocation as the poet of aviation, a writer who transformed his experiences with the Line into best-selling books, among them the evocative *Night Flight; Wind, Sand and Stars;* and *The Little Prince.*

On the eve of his first flight in command of a Latécoère plane, Saint-Exupéry sought the advice of his friend and fellow pilot Henri Guillaumet, who had flown the route from Toulouse to Alicante many times before. "Guillaumet did not teach Spain to me, he made the country my friend," Saint-Exupéry wrote later. The veteran warned the novice about the hazards that lay in ambush—three orange trees near the Guadix field, a nearly invisible brook on another landing strip. A few weeks later Saint-Exupéry was in Africa, riding as a passenger on another pilot's flight to Dakar, when a broken connecting rod sent their craft slamming into a dune with the loss of a wing and the landing gear. Guillaumet, who was flying as escort, dropped down and picked up the mail and the other pilot; Saint-Exupéry was given a gun and told to use it if he was attacked before they could get back for him. The seasoned fliers neglected to tell the eager beginner that they had landed in an area that was free of hostile bands. When Guillaumet returned four hours later, an excited Saint-Exupéry—still clutching his pistol—proudly reported: "They did not come."

Saint-Ex, as the other pilots called him, moved in October 1927 to a new post as manager of the Cape Juby field, a station whose borders were described by one visitor as "water, sand, and shadow." It was also bounded by fear; increased activity by the Moors had inspired an order that no one was to stray more than 500 yards from the fort, and for good reason. André Dubourdieu, playing cards with two fellow fliers one night in the airmen's quarters next to the wall of the fort, saw a rifle barrel suddenly poke through the open window. The pilots immediately doused the oil lamp and raced outside, but their would-be assailant had

Trailed by desert tribesmen and French mail pilots, Saint-Exupéry strolls with Colonel de la Peña, the Spanish governor of Cape Juby, on a tour of the airfield just outside the fort. The diplomatic flier's primary duty at Juby was to smooth Latécoère's relations with the autocratic governor.

vanished in the darkness. Saint-Exupéry's chores as head of this danger spot included negotiating with the Moors, retrieving downed pilots and planes, and soothing the tender sensibilities of the Spanish proprietors—who were growing ever more embarrassed at their inability to control the menacing nomads.

The new manager turned out to be an effective diplomat as well as an imaginative director of the frequent rescue missions. Curious about the culture of "this land where each step makes the heart beat faster," Saint-Exupéry studied Arabic and dressed in loose-fitting Arab-style robes. He cultivated tribesmen who showed any disposition to be friendly, and as his tenure progressed the Moors came gradually to trust him so much that they solicited his advice on such matters as marriages and internal quarrels.

On one occasion he organized a caravan consisting of 11 generally friendly Moors, a mechanic and a camel-drawn cart to transport a replacement engine to a plane that had come down 20 miles from the fort. The Moors, fearful of trespassing on the territory of a rival band, decided to abandon Saint-Exupéry in the desert, but he kept them in line by alternately shaming and bullying them. When a party of raiders showed up, the hired Moors drove them off. Saint-Exupéry got the plane repaired and returned to Cape Juby.

From his convenient perch on the back of a camel—the "stepladder of the desert"—Louis Vidalon, an electrical mechanic, performs repairs on the engine of a Laté 26 mailplane.

Like the other pilots of the Line, Saint-Exupéry dutifully accepted the gospel according to Daurat: The mail, the job, *duty*—were everything. Unlike his comrades, however, Saint-Exupéry could articulate the pilots' creed. The mail was at once "the meditation of a people" and "the dogma of the religion" of the pilots' calling. It did not matter if the letters themselves were nothing more than the jottings of tradesmen or obscure lovers. "The mail is sacred," he declared. "What it contains is of little importance." It was worth all of the sacrifices because the pilots believed in the importance of what they did.

British airmail activity in the immediate postwar years had been far less ambitious and romantic than its French counterpart. Or perhaps it just seemed that way; the British may have suffered from the lack of a widely read chronicler like Saint-Exupéry. The fact was that the several airlines linking England and the Continent carried passengers first and mail sacks second. British postal officials, despite their pioneering experiments in 1911, were somewhat dubious about committing mail to the air; only reluctantly did they permit airmail service between London and Paris—and not until three months after the passenger line between the two capitals began in 1919. And the doubters seemed vindicated: When the airmail finally got under way, the weather immediately closed it down for several days. British leaders, moreover, unlike the French, were disinclined to subsidize private mail lines. Civil aviation, in the words of Secretary of State for Air Winston Churchill, would have to "fly by itself," without assistance from the state. The public apparently was not impressed either; patronage was so scanty that the average mail load in late 1921 was only four to five pounds per flight.

British interest perked up, however, when it became evident that the airmail had a potential for knitting together the strands of a far-flung empire. In early 1919 the Air Ministry sent Royal Air Force ground crews to Africa to construct a chain of landing fields and support facilities between Cairo and Cape Town, on the southern tip of the continent. The crews hacked through jungles and grasslands in the roadless heart of Africa, scraping away 25-foot-high anthills and clearing fields, only to see the jungle vegetation sprout up again a few weeks after they had finished. They had to contract with local chiefs to keep the landing grounds clear. By March 1920 the fields were pronounced ready, and an intrepid pair of pioneering aviators made it all the way to Cape Town after surviving a crack-up in Johannesburg. With that, the Cairo-to-the-Cape airmail project yielded to discretion and halted; there were too many obstacles. The fields were used only sporadically for the next decade, while the displaced ants mounted a counterattack.

Still eager to test their airmail wings, the British shifted their gaze to the Middle East, and in June 1921, RAF de Havillands, both single-engined D.H.9As and twin-engined D.H.10s, began carrying military mail and supplies on an 864-mile route between Cairo and Baghdad. The pilots flew in two- or three-plane convoys along the southeastern shore of the Mediterranean, across Palestine and the northern coast of the Dead Sea to Amman, Trans-Jordan, and then over 500 miles of featureless desert to Baghdad. The main purpose was to give military aviators experience in cross-country flying, but the postal operation was handled so smoothly that civil mail was taken on after a few months. Not that the loads were exactly excessive: One of the fortnightly flights in October carried a total of 57 letters; on a November flight, the number increased, but only to a still-paltry 172.

The long journey over the sandscape between Amman and Baghdad was broken by refueling stops at fields equipped with underground storage tanks hidden from sometimes pesky—but rarely homicidal—bands of Bedouin nomads. To give the pilots something to navigate by in this land without landmarks, the British sent trucks and cars along the route to make a track that the pilots could follow from as much as two miles up. Every 20 miles or so there was a circular furrow enclosing an identifying letter or number to mark the emergency landing fields.

One of the greatest hazards in this barren country was boredom and the mental wanderlust that could seize a pilot whose only reference point was a monotonous line on the sand. A flier who lost the track had to circle until he found it again. Once, a pilot and copilot were traversing a 50-mile-long region of dark lava hills in the desert when they drifted south of their course and over country that neither had seen before. Suddenly the pilot was startled to see a small green valley set amid the hills, with a tidy little village nestled in the midst of the valley. After

Ground crew look over a Latécoère 28 mailplane fitted out with floats and a powerful 650-hp engine for the first nonstop flight across the South Atlantic on May 12-13, 1930. Piloted by Jean Mermoz, the Laté 28 made the 1,900-mile hop from Senegal to Natal in just 19½ hours.

finding his way back to the track and flying on to Baghdad, the pilot excitedly told his friends what he had seen. They did not believe him. His copilot confirmed that he had seen it too, but the other fliers were still not convinced. On his next flight the pilot searched for the mysterious village but could not find it. Neither could anyone else, then or ever.

There were other problems, too. On one occasion, a three-plane convoy ran out of daylight and landed for the night at one of the desert emergency fields. The airmen made themselves comfortable under the wings of the planes and went to sleep. Shortly after dawn they awoke to find that a sudden and inexplicable rainstorm had fallen during the night, in an area where rain was practically unknown. The sand beneath their landing gear had become a quagmire, and it took a full day of frustrating labor to get the planes airborne again.

The rewards of desert flying were the rare glimpses of its beauty that the desert permitted. Pilot Roderic Hill described one such glimpse on a night flight over the Sinai to Cairo: "The clouds had cleared away and had left a turquoise sky. So strong was the moon that the landscape was full of colour, rich though subdued. A faint haze only served to heighten the beauty of the night-filled desert. And I could see the dark and light patterns on the desert dimly glittering."

The RAF eventually installed rudimentary two-way radios in its planes and flew some routes at night. The ease with which the desert accommodated forced landings contributed to an extraordinary safety record: There was not a single pilot fatality in the five years the RAF flew the Baghdad route. Then in 1926 the military yielded the furrowed track and the rest of the desert flyway to Imperial Airways, a two-year-old government-subsidized company that had grown out of the merger of several privately owned British airlines.

Soon this ambitious enterprise—which carried passengers as well as mail—was busily extending the old Baghdad airmail line on to India. By 1935, after a few false starts, Imperial was flying regularly from London all the way to Australia, thus forging a final link in a grandiose scheme to tie the entire British Empire together with airmail routes (pages 165-167). The French, meanwhile, had somewhat upstaged the British by conquering the South Atlantic and fulfilling Pierre Latécoère's similarly ambitious dream of connecting Europe and Africa to South America.

From the start, Latécoère had envisioned an 8,000-mile-long mail route running from Toulouse to Tierra del Fuego, simultaneously a tribute to French aeronautical accomplishment and a boon to French commerce. He had intended ultimately to use seaplanes to cross the South Atlantic between Dakar and Natal in Brazil, and from there to convey the mail the 2,900 miles to Buenos Aires and, later, to Patagonia and across the Andes to Chile. But just as this bold prospect was nearing reality, Latécoère lost control of the Line.

Latécoère's most vexing problems in building a mail route in South America were not aeronautical but rather political and financial. The

One man's airmail odyssey

In 1932, Paris illustrator Georges Hamel, who was known professionally as Géo Ham, sent an airmail letter to a friend in Santiago, Chile. The letter got him to thinking: It would travel for more than a week through all weathers, flown by brave men willing to risk their lives to carry the mail halfway around the world. Ham decided he wanted to get to know these heroes of the French Aéropostale by traveling with them along the same route his letter had taken. But since most of the planes were not fitted to carry passengers, he had to endure almost the entire trip in the mail compartments.

Over Africa he roasted by day and froze by night. Arriving at the continent's westernmost point, he transferred to a swift mail boat and was whisked to South America in 96 hours. There he resumed his flight, traveling from Natal, on Brazil's northern coast, to Rio de Janeiro and Buenos Aires before being lofted over the Andes by Henri Guillaumet, one of the most celebrated Aéropostale pilots. The plane was caught in cross currents, jolted in every direction and whipped by wind. Ham, squeezed among the mailbags, clung to the fuselage with fingers numb from the 35°-below-zero cold.

The outcome of the 21,000-mile journey was an article for the magazine, *L'Illustration,* highlighted by Ham's watercolors, six of which are reproduced here and on the following pages, showing what it was like to fly with the airmail.

Under the eye of an armed guard, blue-veiled Moorish tribesmen look on as mailbags are unloaded from a Laté 26 monoplane at the Aéropostale outpost at Cape Juby, in the Spanish Sahara.

His waistband bristling with decorative daggers, a Moorish interpreter snuggles among the mailbags and other cargo on the night flight Ham took down the African coast from Cape Juby to Dakar.

Flying the flags of France and Brazil, the mail boat Aéropostale II plows through heavy seas as it approaches the coast of South America after the four-day passage across the Atlantic from Africa.

As city lights flicker in the distance, the ▷ Aéropostale mailplane approaches Sugar Loaf, the rock formation that marks the entrance to Rio de Janeiro Bay.

Its wheel-mounted landing lights seeming to trace lines through the night sky, a Laté 26 bearing Ham swoops toward the illuminated landing field at Mendoza, Argentina, where the mail was transferred to a high-flying Potez 25 biplane for the journey across the Andes.

Bound for Santiago, the powerful little Potez wings over the snow-capped peaks of the Andes. Ham, his leather flying suit insulated with layers of newspaper to ward off the cold, was secured in the mail compartment with ropes to protect him during the turbulent passage.

political obstacle was the need for cooperation from the governments of Brazil, Uruguay and Argentina. He cleared this hurdle with the aid of Vicente Almonacid, an Argentinian pilot who had flown for France during the War. Almonacid smoothed the way for a series of 1925 test flights that connected Rio de Janeiro with Recife in the north and Buenos Aires in the south. It was the more painful financial dilemma that brought Latécoère down. Overextension had exhausted his capital, and in April 1927 he sold out to Marcel Bouilloux-Lafont, a wealthy French businessman with extensive holdings in South America. Bouilloux-Lafont changed the company's name to Aéropostale, and Latécoère returned to building planes in Toulouse.

The new owner directed the construction of needed airfields, recruited local people to staff them and created subsidiary companies in each country. He also summoned Jean Mermoz to be chief pilot in South America, but it took a while for the imperious proprietor and his proud subordinate to understand each other. Bouilloux-Lafont sent word one day that he wanted Mermoz to fly him on a private trip, whereupon Mermoz stormed into the office and announced: "I am a pilot of the Line, do you understand? I am here to carry the mail, to open air routes, and not to be employed as the house chauffeur." Mermoz prevailed.

Regular flights on the long route between Natal and Buenos Aires began in November 1927 in a new Latécoère-built plane called the Laté 25. Powered by a single 450-horsepower Renault engine, the plane had a much greater range than its predecessors and also boasted space for four passengers—if such could be found—in addition to the mail pouches. Since the seaplane that would provide the crucial transoceanic link in the chain was not yet available, Aéropostale accepted the French government's offer of four obsolete destroyers for ferrying the mail between Africa and South America. The first planes carrying transatlantic mail took off from Toulouse and Buenos Aires in March 1928, but a combination of mishaps and misunderstandings delayed the South America-bound consignment; it arrived at about the same time as the shipborne mail. A month later Mermoz initiated night flights on the South American coastal route to speed service, despite the absence of airway beacons such as those used in the United States.

The Line added a spur to Paraguay in early 1929, but the most formidable test on the South American mainland was passage across the Andean mountain chain to Chile. Most of the Andes passes were higher than the 13,000-foot ceiling of the Aéropostale planes. Mermoz and a mechanic named Collenot were sent out to probe the range for passes that the company's planes could negotiate safely. Caught in a downdraft in one such flight, they were forced down on the rocky top of a steep-sided plateau at an elevation of 12,000 feet. Mermoz found that the plane was still flyable, but he also discovered that there was not a level clearing large enough for a takeoff; they would have to hike out.

For two days Mermoz and Collenot explored the mountaintop in search of a way down, but the cliffs just beneath the plateau were so steep that they dared not try a descent. Now the only chance they had left was to get into the plane and roar off the edge of the precipice, gambling that the craft would gain enough speed in falling to respond to the controls. It was an all-or-nothing risk—if it failed they would be pulverized on the rocks below.

Mermoz and Collenot moved the plane into position and jumped in. Then the pilot weaved and bounced over the boulders and careened off the edge of the cliff. The plane fell like a wounded eagle until Mermoz suddenly felt it responding to his controls. He barely cleared a peak dead ahead of him; then he saw the Chilean plain and deliverance.

A few months later the company acquired several Potez 25 biplanes that had a ceiling of 19,000 feet, and regular mail flights across the mountains became possible. Mermoz and Guillaumet opened the scheduled route from Buenos Aires to Santiago, Chile, in July 1929.

A few months later, they were joined in South America by Saint-

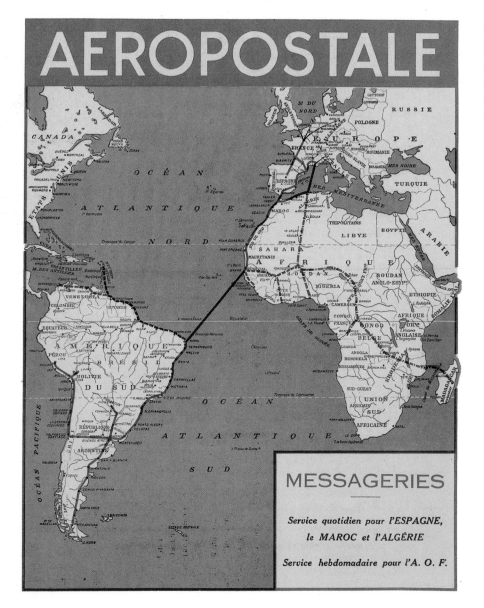

A 1930 French map shows the scheduled mail route (solid line) of Aéropostale, the direct descendant of the Latécoère airline, with its links to three continents. Proposed mail routes are indicated by broken lines; these failed to materialize after Aéropostale suffered financial reverses.

In bold, rectilinear Art Deco style, an early 1930s poster designed to draw business for Aéropostale in Argentina depicts the airline as arrow fleet and lists in Spanish the countries and continents the French mail carrier had expanded to serve.

AEROPOSTA

INDICADOR

LINEAS AEREAS EN LA REP. ARGENTINA Y ENTRE LA ARGENTINA
CHILE - PARAGUAY - BRASIL - AFRICA Y EUROPA

Exupéry, whose exemplary tour of duty at Africa's cheerless Cape Juby airmail station had ended earlier in the year. (On his return home to await reassignment, Saint-Exupéry had been surprised to be rewarded with the Legion of Honor; the citation commended ''his zeal, his devotion, and his noble unselfishness'' in the cause of French aviation.) It was not long before the poetic French pilot discovered for himself that flying in South America presented hazards undreamed of in the barren wastes of Africa. Not least among them was the violent pampero, a wind that swept out of the Andes and raked the southern Argentine coast at speeds of up to 150 miles an hour.

Saint-Exupéry collided with a pampero on a flight down the coast to the Patagonian town of Comodoro Rivadavia. For several minutes he bucked the cyclonic wind and went nowhere. ''My wings had ceased to nibble into the outline of the earth,'' he wrote later. ''I could see the earth buckle, pivot—but it stayed put. The plane was skidding as if on a

France's noble carriers

During the 1920s and '30s, French mail-planes regularly traversed some of the world's most forbidding terrain. Two of Aéropostale's best-known aircraft, beloved by the adventurers who flew them, are presented here, in scale and wearing their original colors. The dates represent the years the planes first flew.

The Latécoère 28 *(above)* plied the desert route between Casablanca and Dakar in North Africa. It was one of the fastest airliners of its day and, when fitted out as a seaplane, flew the first transatlantic airmail in 1930. The Potez 25, used on the Aéropostale line's South American routes, could climb to 19,000 feet and was nearly indestructible: Pilot Henri Guillaumet's Potez *(right),* which crashed in the Andes during a snowstorm, was recovered almost intact a few months later. Repaired, it continued to fly the mail for many years afterward.

LATÉCOÈRE 28 (1929)
Powered by a 500-hp Hispano-Suiza engine, the Latécoère 28 was a high-wing monoplane with room for eight passengers. Its top speed of 158 mph and 621-mile range helped it set several world records.

POTEZ 25 (1925)
Henri Guillaumet's Potez 25 had a top speed of 136 mph and a range of 310 miles. First exhibited in 1924 at the Paris Air Show, the Potez 25 became one of the most widely used planes of its day and some 4,000 were eventually built.

Henri Guillaumet, who ultimately made 343 flights over the Andes for Aéropostale, chomps his cigar in the cockpit of his plane. When he later survived a crash at 17,000 feet during a June blizzard in 1930, he became, in the words of Saint-Exupéry, "the author of his own miracle."

toothless cogwheel.'' Moments later he was abruptly lofted 1,500 feet and then ''spat out to sea by a monstrous cough, vomited out of my valley as from the mouth of a howitzer.'' Saint-Exupéry felt as if he were ''clinging to the tip of a monstrous whip that was cracking over the sea.'' Gripping the wheel so tightly that his hands went numb, he fought to hold the plane steady and to keep the coast in view. He did not know that the ribs on his wings were beginning to loosen and his control cables were almost sliced through. He, too, was weakening—''the strength and will oozing out of me,'' he recalled. But after struggling for more than two hours he gained the shore, turned south in the shelter of a long cliff and proceeded to his destination.

Appointed chief of Aéropostale's operations in Argentina, Saint-Exupéry soon extended the mail routes down through Patagonia to Río Gallegos, near the Strait of Magellan. Then the men of Aéropostale turned to the Atlantic Ocean itself, the only barrier still unconquered.

Once again Mermoz played the leading role. Latécoère had produced a still larger and more reliable long-distance machine in his Laté 28, and Daurat had suggested the addition of a 650-horsepower Hispano-Suiza engine and floats for the transatlantic voyage. With a navigator and a radio operator, Mermoz took off from Senegal in the high-wing craft on May 12, 1930, with 270 pounds of mail and a 27-hour fuel supply. Aéropostale ships were stationed along the route.

As darkness overtook him about a third of the way across, Mermoz encountered a remarkable phenomenon—endless columns of enormous waterspouts rose from the sea like pillars roofed by storm clouds. Mermoz guided the plane through the tornado-like columns with no consequences more serious than a temporarily flooded cockpit. Early the next morning he touched down in the harbor at Natal, having covered the 1,900 miles in 19 hours and 35 minutes. The mail was transferred to another Aéropostale plane and rushed on to Buenos Aires, where it arrived only four days after leaving France.

Mermoz' triumph was marred by the news that three Aéropostale men flying to welcome him had drowned when their plane was forced down in the Río de la Plata off Montevideo. The Frenchmen had given the craft's two life preservers to their two Brazilian passengers, one of whom survived to salute their heroism.

Aéropostale suffered another setback when Mermoz' attempt to fly the west-to-east transatlantic route in July came to grief 350 miles short of Africa owing to a broken oil line; the crewmen were picked up by ship, but their plane was lost. Regular mail flights across the South Atlantic would have to wait a few more years for an airplane that was equal to the job.

There were also problems in the Andes, and with the onset of the Southern Hemisphere winter in late May the always hazardous flights across the mountains became even more perilous. The Andes route was the domain of the stolid and unprepossessing Henri Guillaumet. He had already made 95 successful trips over the range when he ascended from Santiago on Friday, June 13, 1930, and headed into a blizzard that blocked his course to Mendoza, Argentina. Searching for a break in the storm, he nosed his Potez 25 into a high valley flanked by peaks reaching to 20,000 feet, but a powerful downdraft pinned him below the mountaintops; he was trapped. Guillaumet flew for two hours around a frozen lake on the valley floor before he ran out of fuel and glided to a dead-stick landing on the snow, breaking his propeller as the plane flipped upside down.

Jean Macaigne, an Aéropostale radioman, was in Buenos Aires when he heard that Guillaumet was missing. "We were all convinced that we would never see him again," he recalled later. "We immediately left to search for him, but we did not see him. The Potez 25 was painted white, which made it hard to distinguish on snow." Saint-Exupéry flew up from Patagonia to join the search.

Guillaumet had gone down in one of the Andes' most rugged and isolated areas in the coldest season of the year. A Chilean Army officer

Beside her well sits the Indian woman onto whose farm (right) a grizzled Guillaumet stumbled after his five-day struggle against death in the Andes. Taking him for a bandit, she was ready to flee on her donkey when her son, who had heard news of the lost airman, cried, "El aviador!"

told Saint-Exupéry that even if his friend survived the landing he would never live through the nights, when temperatures plunged to 20° below zero. Indeed, when Guillaumet climbed out of his plane he was knocked down by the wind; when he got up he was bowled over again. He dug a pit in the snow under the fuselage and crawled into it, making himself as warm as he could amid the mailbags. He waved frantically when he saw a search plane pass, but the pilot was too high to spot him. During the next two days he finished the small supply of food he had with him as he lay in his snow foxhole waiting for the storm to subside.

On the third day Guillaumet started to walk out. He would have to make his way on foot over the ice-covered mountain walls that his plane had not been able to clear. Laboriously he inched his way upward, falling frequently, kicking holes in the ice with his boots. At one point he toppled 150 feet into a ravine. He desperately wanted to give up, and once he decided that he could go no farther. Then he thought of his wife and the insurance she would collect, and remembered that payment was withheld for four years in cases where no body was found. He refused to let himself sleep for fear he would not wake up. Gradually his hands became numb, then his feet. He cut his shoes open to ease the pressure on his swollen feet. He mushed on, dimly realizing that he was growing delirious; he kept forgetting things when he stopped to rest—a glove, his watch, a knife, a compass, the very things he needed most.

Guillaumet struggled on for three days and nights before he finally got over the peaks that imprisoned him. On his fourth day of walking and climbing he finally came upon a woman tending goats on the outskirts of a mountain village. The sight of grass excited him so that he fell to his knees and munched it as an animal would. The startled woman first ran, then warily returned to take him into her stone hut and summon help. When Saint-Exupéry flew to the area to greet Guillaumet soon afterward he was aghast at his comrade's appearance—"burned to a crisp" by the sun, his face "splotched and swollen like an overripe fruit that has been repeatedly dropped on the ground."

Guillaumet's ordeal was one of the greatest survival stories in the history of aviation, and his rescue was celebrated both by his fellow pilots and by the Latin Americans.

That marked a sort of peak in Aéropostale's fortunes. By early 1931 the Line was once more in grave financial straits, and Bouilloux-Lafont became embroiled in a scandal involving forged documents and charges that bureaucrats had been bribed to withhold the Aéropostale subsidy. For a while the pilots worked without pay; then in 1932 Aéropostale was liquidated, and the boldest, most imaginative airmail venture in history flamed out. A year later its remnants were merged with other French airlines into Air France. And with the transition to large national airlines such as Air France, the wide-ranging German Lufthansa *(pages 136-145)* and Britain's Imperial Airways, there was little place for routes devoted primarily to mail. Saint-Exupéry's "meditation of a people" had become just another part of the load. ◥◥

Rescuers right Guillaumet's Potez 25, which flipped over on its back when the propeller struck the snow. The pilot was attempting to make a forced landing on the shores of a volcano-warmed lake, one of the few flat sites in the mountain landscape.

Lufthansa's conquest of the world

Unlike Great Britain and France, which established international airmail routes to link the scattered countries of their empires, Germany began flying the mail beyond Europe after it had lost its empire. As a punitive measure after World War I, the Allies had forced the defeated nation to relinquish its colonies. Without colonial markets as outlets for its manufactured goods and as sources of raw materials, Germany could recover its power and prestige only by rebuilding its international trade. And in order to vie successfully with other nations in a worldwide marketplace, Germany would have to speed commercial documents and payments over long distances by flying the mail.

Renowned for its air-mindedness even before World War I, postwar Germany undertook this vital project with great energy. At one time, as many as 37 German airlines competed ruthlessly for airmail routes and government subsidies, but in 1926 the government consolidated its airmail efforts by founding a single national airline, Deutsche Luft Hansa.

With the creation of Luft Hansa (contracted to Lufthansa in 1934), Germany began to expand its airmail network in earnest. In South America, where many German immigrants engaged in the lucrative import-export business with the fatherland, German entrepreneurs had already established several domestic airlines; now these carriers became Lufthansa subsidiaries or associates.

To connect South America's services with Europe, Lufthansa surveyed a route from Germany to the Canary Islands in 1929 *(right)*. Then, using seaplanes with catapult ships as refueling bases, the airline pressed on across the South Atlantic. German seaplanes and catapult ships also conquered the broader and more tempestuous North Atlantic, conducting experimental flights to New York.

Other German business interests attracted Lufthansa to Asia. Here, the airline's Chinese subsidiary, Eurasia, pioneered mail routes that were to be the eastern segments of a service from Berlin to Shanghai and Tokyo. The tremendous obstacles encountered in flying the mail to three continents—and the techniques adopted to overcome them—are depicted on the following pages.

Excited spectators gather around a Lufthansa Arado VI mailplane after its successful test flight from Seville, Spain, to Tenerife in the Canary Islands on December 5, 1929.

137

Mapping out mail routes in South America

Daunted by South America's dense jungles, German pilots of Lufthansa's subsidiaries and associates began by flying the mail along the coastline. Pushing on into the interior, they discovered that the broad network of rivers provided better landing areas than the rugged airstrips. Finally, in 1935, Lufthansa's Brazilian associate crossed the perilous Andes, spanning the wealthy continent.

A Junkers F 13 of Lufthansa's Colombian associate pauses during its exploration of South America's Pacific coast.

Braving the interior, a Junkers G 24 equipped with pontoons alights on one of Brazil's many waterways.

Setting off from a Peruvian airfield, a Junkers 52 prepares to negotiate the Andes' narrow passes.

A seaplane touches down off Brazil to rendezvous with an eastward-bound liner.

Launched from a ship off Africa's west coast, a Dornier 18 heads for South America.

Help from ships to bridge the Atlantic

At first, German seaplanes from South America ventured only 200 miles into the Atlantic, to transfer their mail to German passenger liners bound for Europe. Then, in 1929, a time-saving innovation was introduced: The German liner *Bremen (below)* launched a mailplane from a catapult on her bow as she approached New York. Soon specialized catapult ships were stationed up and down the Atlantic to act as mobile fueling stations for ocean-hopping Lufthansa planes.

A Heinkel 12 loaded with mail soars from the upper deck of the ocean liner Bremen 300 miles from New York City.

Opening up the Far East

In attempting to fly the mail across Asia, Lufthansa and its Chinese subsidiary, Eurasia, encountered a vast continent of mountains, deserts and jungles. Nevertheless, German pilots managed to conduct survey flights along two trans-Asiatic routes—a northern route, crossing Siberia and the Gobi Desert, and a southern route, traversing the Middle East, northern India and Thailand.

Equipped with balloon tires for use on the primitive airfields in China, a Lufthansa Junkers W 33 takes off from Lanchow.

A Eurasia aircraft wings over the mountainous terrain of northwestern China.

Awaiting his connecting flight, a German pilot camps out in the Chinese wilderness.

Rescuing a mailplane in China

Grueling terrain was not the only problem that Eurasia faced in carrying mail, freight and passengers in the Far East. During Japan's occupation of eastern China in the late 1930s, Japanese aircraft attacked even civilian planes. The Junkers 52 shown here was shot down in April 1939; repairing the craft—and converting a mountainside into an emergency runway—took six months.

Chinese workers struggle to dislodge a Junkers 52 that crashed into the side of a mountain after being machine-gunned by Japanese fighter-bombers.

Laborers set out to dig a makeshift runway into the mountain slope. More than 800 workers excavated some 52,000 cubic yards of earth from the site.

With its right wheel only 10 feet from the edge of the cliff, the repaired Junkers is readied for takeoff from the completed runway.

5

Keepers of a proud tradition

The ground crewmen at Maywood Field outside of Chicago beamed their searchlight at the evening sky and stared anxiously upward. The mailplane from St. Louis was up there somewhere—they could hear the lonesome whine of its Liberty engine—but plane and field were cut off from each other by a layer of fog 800 feet thick that had crept over much of the northern Midwest. In the previous few hours three other mailplanes had been forced to come down short of their destinations. The pilot of the St. Louis plane and the Maywood crewmen searched for each other from their opposite sides of the fog, but all they could see was mist. After a few minutes the drone of the engine faded, then disappeared. Residents of the nearby town of Oak Park heard the plane circling for about an hour longer before the noise stopped. It was September 16, 1926.

The pilot, 24-year-old Charles A. Lindbergh, was flying the St. Louis-to-Chicago route for the Robertson Aircraft Corporation, one of a number of private companies that had won contracts to carry mail after the Post Office began closing down its own airmail operations in 1926. When he hit fog after taking off from Peoria on his final leg to Chicago, his first impulse had been to drop a flare and land on a farm. But when he pulled on the flare's release lever, nothing happened. Then he decided to fly on toward Maywood and look for a hole in the mist. Now he turned west, hoping to spot a beacon on the transcontinental airway; this, too, proved futile. He was running out of both options and time.

A few minutes later the engine sputtered, telling him that his main fuel tank was empty, and he switched to his reserve tank. He had 20 minutes of flying time left. He decided to parachute when the reserve tank ran dry, but suddenly he spied a dim light through the murk. He dropped down to 1,200 feet and tried the flare again; this time he got the release mechanism to work. The flare dropped and ignited, but the scene of unbroken mist it illuminated put an end to his moment of hope. He pulled the stick back and climbed, banking away from the dull glow that marked a town and toward the blackness of open country. He had reached 5,000 feet when the engine quit again; Lindbergh unbuckled his safety belt and plunged over the side. After waiting a few seconds he pulled the rip cord, and the canopy of his parachute blossomed above him. Then he heard a sound he did not expect—an airplane engine.

The plane was his own de Havilland, and it was headed right for him. He anxiously watched the plane grow larger and larger and then pass

In fur-lined flight suits, chief pilot Charles Lindbergh (center) and colleagues Thomas Nelson (left) and Philip Love stand ready to fly the mail between St. Louis and Chicago for the Robertson Aircraft Corporation. Robertson was one of the first private firms to operate under a government mail contract, in 1926.

about 100 yards away, spiraling toward the ground at the same rate as the flier in his chute. He knew what had happened: He had neglected to shut off the ignition switch, and when he jumped the plane had nosed downward, sending the remaining fuel into the carburetor and propelling the plane into pilotless flight. Lindbergh watched helplessly as the de Havilland circled and made another pass at him, still descending at the same rate as his chute. But this time it missed him by a slightly wider margin. The plane spiraled by him four more times before he landed in a cornfield north of Ottawa, Illinois. Unhurt, he picked himself up and promptly encountered a carload of farmers hunting for him and the plane. Lindbergh found his wrecked plane at the edge of another cornfield; the mail was undamaged, and he took it to the nearest post office.

Lindbergh's harrowing experience was front-page news in the next day's *Chicago Tribune,* which identified him as Carl A. Lindbergh. Not until the following spring would the young pilot transform himself—through a 33½-hour transatlantic flight—into a world celebrity. For now, he was a relatively obscure mail pilot, scarcely distinguishable from the scores of other members of that closely knit and elite fraternity.

Like so many of the best American aviators, Lindbergh had gravitated naturally to mail flying: "To be a pilot of the night mail appeared the summit of ambition for a flier," he wrote subsequently. Late in 1925, following stints as a barnstormer and military aviation cadet, he had signed on as chief pilot for Robertson Aircraft. Operated by the brothers William and Frank Robertson of St. Louis, the company had been the successful bidder for the airmail route linking St. Louis with Chicago by way of Springfield and Peoria.

The Post Office paid mail contractors such as the Robertsons up to 80 per cent of the revenue from the mail they carried. A number of the private lines moved quickly to boost their profits by toting passengers as well as mail sacks, but the Robertson company and a few others—among them the Dickinson line in Illinois, Wisconsin and Minnesota, and Walter Varney's desert-and-mountain enterprise in the Pacific Northwest—carried on the traditions of the United States Air Mail Service by concentrating on mail alone, at least for the first few years.

Lindbergh had played a major role in launching the Robertson mail operation, choosing the nine plots of Illinois prairie that served as emergency fields along the 278-mile route. When service was inaugurated, on April 15, 1926, he made a morning trip from Chicago to St. Louis and returned to Chicago in the afternoon, pausing long enough at Springfield to endure a speech by the postmaster and the full-throated admiration of some 5,000 airmail and aviation enthusiasts who had paraded to the field in a mile-long caravan of automobiles.

But the public enthusiasm, which had produced 413 pounds of mail on the first day's flights out of Springfield, proved short-lived. Within a few days the canvas mail sacks were riding almost empty in the forward compartments of the Robertson de Havillands; according to Lindbergh, the sacks often outweighed the letters inside them. Consumer indifference was nothing new in the airmail business, of course, but now it was private enterprise that was feeling the sting. Even at best, the Robertsons were just scrimping along. The line's fleet of four D.H.4s had been acquired as Army surplus for $100 each, then rebuilt in the company shop in St. Louis; the route lacked such niceties as runway lights and beacons for night flying. Operating expenses at Robertson were "incredibly low," Lindbergh observed, but revenue was even lower.

As the days grew shorter in September, the three Robertson pilots—Lindbergh and his 23-year-old colleagues Philip Love and Thomas Nelson—were regularly finishing their afternoon flights in the dark, guided by the lights in farmhouse windows. The number of forced landings increased as the season advanced—Nelson once came down a dozen times to knock ice from his wings while en route to St. Louis—but the Robertson airmen managed to avoid serious damage to themselves or their planes. Then, one evening in early November, Lindbergh was flying 20 minutes north of Springfield when he ran out of light.

Almost immediately, he found himself flying through a storm that blotted out the lights below. He tried to climb above it but found snow in the higher altitudes. Unable to make his scheduled stop at Peoria, he flew on toward Chicago, hoping to outrun the weather, but the snow that way was even heavier. He turned back for Peoria. Descending to about 400 feet, he released his only flare, but its parachute snagged on the tail skid and the flare plummeted to earth like a fireball. For the second time in six weeks Lindbergh was reduced to just one piece of emergency equipment—his own parachute—with nothing but clouds beneath him. He climbed to 14,000 feet, looking for the stars; if he could see them, he thought, he would not mind leaping into the storm.

With memories of his previous jump still fresh in his mind, Lindbergh was careful to switch off the ignition. Then he dived out of the cockpit and pulled the rip cord. This time, the plane did not follow him down. For several minutes he floated silently through the snow, which turned to rain as he neared the ground. He landed on a barbed-wire fence a few miles west of Bloomington, Illinois. After searching in vain for his downed plane, he trekked a mile and a half to the nearest village and caught a train to Chicago. He returned the next day, found the wrecked de Havilland and retrieved the mail.

With the loss of this second aircraft, the Robertson fleet was reduced to only two airplanes, a fact that was brought home forcefully to a pilot named Harlan "Bud" Gurney soon afterward. Gurney was sent with one of the two remaining D.H.4s to take a photographer up for an aerial survey of the Missouri River valley. Bill Robertson told him pointedly that if anything happened to his plane the line would have only one left and would lose its mail contract.

Gurney was cruising at 15,000 feet when the photographer, in the front cockpit, accidentally closed the throttle. When Gurney reopened it the engine backfired, igniting an oil line. Gurney switched off the fuel and went into a sideslip to keep the flames away from the cockpit. "We

spiraled down with black smoke trailing behind us," he remembered. "Fifteen thousand feet is a long, long way when you're sideslipping in a burning D.H." At last he was able to put the blazing plane down on a field in a small town. Gurney and the photographer leaped out and started running. "I turned back just as the wing tank blew," Gurney said. "The wings just folded in and it exploded. I was sick."

He trudged disconsolately to a telephone to report the grim news to Robertson, who asked if the plane had been in the air or on the ground when it blew up. When Gurney replied that the plane had been on the ground, Robertson wanted to know if the photographer had managed to snap any pictures of the burning craft. Told that he had, Gurney recalled, Robertson "whooped and said, 'Don't worry about a thing, we're insured against a plane destroyed by fire on the ground.' Darned if he didn't collect $25,000 from the insurance company, enough to put him right back in business."

Despite this disaster-turned-bonanza, the Robertson line's operations remained precarious, though the pilots' work became a little easier with the installation of a network of beacons between St. Louis and Chicago in the winter of 1927. Lindbergh flew the first run on the lighted airway on a night when the ground temperature was 19 below zero. (Soon

Charles Lindbergh's wrecked mailplane draws a small crowd to the Illinois pasture where it crashed on the stormy evening of November 3, 1926. Lucky Lindy, making his second emergency jump in six weeks, landed on a barbed-wire fence that did no more damage than rip his borrowed bearskin flying suit.

afterward, he left the company to devote his full attention to preparations for his transatlantic flight, which would transform American attitudes toward flying and affect every aspect of the aviation industry.) Robertson Aircraft closed its first year of mail flying with an impressive performance record: Ninety-seven per cent of its scheduled flights had been completed. But the operation was still losing money, and the Robertsons eventually sold their line to another company that later became a part of American Airlines.

The Robertson brothers may have had their share of troubles, but the record for the shortest and rockiest career among the early airmail contractors clearly belonged to Charles Dickinson, a luxuriantly whiskered, 70-year-old Chicagoan who had won the contract for the route between Chicago and Minneapolis-St. Paul. Dickinson had made a fortune in the seed business and then helped Emil M. "Matty" Laird build commercial and racing planes. He inaugurated his mail line on June 7, 1926, with a fleet of five planes—four Laird biplanes and an enclosed-cabin craft fashioned from the carcasses of other planes.

The Dickinson line's opening day was a harbinger of woes to come. Rain, hail and gale-force winds shoved the relatively small Dickinson planes all over the north-country sky. Only two of the six flights between Chicago and the Twin Cities via Milwaukee and La Crosse, Wisconsin, reached their goal. Pilot Daniel Kiser had to make an emergency landing when the wind ripped part of the linen cover off one wing; Henry Keller was grounded twice with a broken gas line; Matty Laird, flying in one of his own planes, ran out of light at La Crosse and could not go on.

The veteran Elmer Partridge, an aviation pioneer who had been a pilot since before World War I, was flying the hybrid plane, the final Dickinson craft to challenge the storm that day. Charles Dickinson had tried to dissuade the 46-year-old Partridge from taking off from Chicago in the morning, but the pilot had managed to bring his homemade plane into Minneapolis without mishap. A few hours later Partridge ascended again for the return trip to Chicago, but he was caught in violent air turbulence near the Mississippi River at Mendota and thrown into a spin. The craft recovered briefly, then turned nose down and plunged to the ground. Partridge was dead when a bystander reached the plane.

Two weeks later, after two of his pilots refused to fly until "safer and faster ships" were provided, the elderly Dickinson climbed into the cockpit and carried the mail to Minneapolis himself. "These fliers have more temperament than an opera singer," the old man grumbled. As if skittish pilots and brittle planes were not burden enough, Dickinson also had to contend with four-legged trespassers—cows, sheep, pigs, goats and donkeys—grazing on the Minneapolis landing strip. He complained to the police chief after pilot Bill Brock was forced to land "close enough to a Jersey cow to milk her."

By mid-August Dickinson had had enough. Blaming unspecified "circumstances and conditions"—doubtless including the facts that he was losing money, his mail fleet had been reduced to a single plane and all

but one of his pilots had quit—he posted the 45-day notice needed to cancel his contract. The Post Office invited new bids, and on October 1 the route was taken over by the newly organized Northwest Airways.

Like Dickinson and the Robertsons, airmail contractor Walter T. Varney of San Mateo, California, was a flier himself. The operator of a flying school and an air taxi service, Varney was the lone bidder for what appeared to be the least promising of the early contract routes, a 435-mile track between Elko, Nevada, and Pasco, Washington, two remote, sage-fringed cow towns. This was called "the nowhere route," but Varney knew that Pasco was a key railhead with overnight train connections to the major cities of the Northwest. At Pasco, his planes could pick up mail from Seattle, Portland, Spokane and Tacoma and rush it to Elko, a stop on the transcontinental airmail route. The main obstacles on Varney's route, which had a midway stop at Boise, Idaho, were the sparsely peopled terrain and a daunting succession of mountains, high desert, canyons and more mountains. On one stretch between Elko and Boise the gap between telephones was said to be 100 miles.

While its engine revs up, a Varney Air Lines Swallow waits to take off from Pasco, Washington, on the first contract mail flight to Boise, Idaho, and Elko, Nevada. Cheering on pilot Leon Cuddeback that April 1926 day were some 2,500 spectators, including cowboys atop a stagecoach (left).

At Boise, Varney chief pilot Cuddeback is photographed with the pride of the airline—a modified Swallow with a 200-hp air-cooled Wright Whirlwind engine mounted behind a modern metal propeller. The new engine replaced a balky 150-hp Curtiss K-6.

To traverse this demanding country Varney assembled an unimposing fleet of six Swallow biplanes equipped with 150-horsepower engines, but the underpowered Swallows and the rugged mountain-and-desert landscape were a mismatch from the start. Pilot Joseph Taff was ferrying a plane to Pasco a day before the line's official opening when the engine died as he neared the field. His rough landing on a sandy sagebrush plain damaged the plane and broke Taff's nose—the first of nine such fractures he would suffer. On the next morning, April 6, 1926, some 2,500 people and a handful of uneasy horses watched Varney Air Lines pilot Leon Cuddeback take off from Pasco with 200 pounds of mail—much of it from the metropolises of the Northwest—destined to be transferred at Elko to the eastbound government planes that were still flying the demanding transcontinental route. At Boise, where the town declared a holiday, the cargo was enhanced by a lumpy sack of Idaho potatoes, a gift from local American Legionnaires to President Calvin Coolidge in Washington. Cuddeback flew on to Elko amid strong winds and thunderstorms, arriving safely in the early afternoon. He described the weather conditions to Franklin Rose, who took off a short time later on the Elko-to-Pasco inaugural.

Rose headed north and passed over Tuscarora, about 75 miles away. Then the wind Cuddeback had warned against blew Rose off course in the lonely country north of Tuscarora, and a defective compass frustrated his attempts to correct his heading. He was 75 miles off course when he landed on a muddy patch of ground just north of the Idaho-Nevada line. The plane was undamaged, but its wheels were mired in the mud. Marooned in a land where next-door neighbors lived 25 miles apart, Rose hiked off to find help. When he failed to arrive in Boise by 6 o'clock the Varney men there began calling the few ranches along the route that had telephones, but no one had seen him. They decided not to tell Rose's wife, who was ill at their home in Piedmont, California.

The manhunt that began the next day used planes, cars, and men on horseback and afoot. Ranchers and Indians ranged the roadless desert while government and private planes circled above. The other Varney pilots agreed grudgingly to continue flying their scheduled mail routes rather than take part in the search. Rose, meanwhile, finally found a ranch and borrowed a horse. He rode 30 miles to a house that had a telephone and called Boise, 48 hours after he had vanished.

By the end of his first week in the mail business Walter Varney realized that his Swallows' 150-horsepower Curtiss engines were too weak. He asked for permission to suspend flying for 60 days so that he could replace them with 200-horsepower Wright Whirlwinds, and the Post Office consented. Installation of the new engines was followed by a week of trial runs before operations resumed in June. But low-powered engines were only one hindrance among the many that impeded Varney's company; another was the lack of beacons or landing lights. Ground crewmen handled this shortcoming with reckless ingenuity. When they heard a plane arriving in darkness, they splashed gasoline at one end of the runway and lit it, then switched on the headlights of an automobile parked at the far end of the landing strip. The pilot glided in over the flames and rolled to a landing short of the car. Night landings were particularly adventurous at the Boise field, which was bordered by high trees, power lines and the cables of an electric trolley.

The severe winter weather that had plagued government mail aviators in the mountainous West was another hazard. On a flight in January 1927, pilot George Buck flew through sleet and snow so thick that he unbuckled his safety belt and stood up in the cockpit to try to see past his ice-glazed windshield. When his goggles iced up, he removed them, only to have his face battered by chunks of ice thrown back at him by the propeller. The next day, on a flight from Pasco to Boise, Buck was forced down by fog on the western side of the Blue Mountains, and he sent the mail on by train.

Varney lost money steadily until the Post Office changed the system for paying mail contractors. Formerly, the lines had received a percentage of the postage on the letters that they carried. Now, they were paid a fixed rate per pound of mail per mile, which almost doubled Varney's proceeds and buoyed many of the other contractors as well. The 38-year-old Varney also helped himself with his gift for promotion. He convinced chambers of commerce along his route that they should do business by airmail, then designed a one-ounce message sheet he called an Air-O-Gram. He persuaded so many letter writers in the region to use it—and pay the extra airmail rate—that the entire staff of the Boise Post Office was rewarded with promotion to a higher salary grade.

Residents of the Northwest enjoyed the exuberant style of the Varney line. "The Varney fliers have won the hearts of Boise people by their spirit, their enthusiasm and their effort to show that a contract service could start on time," an Idaho paper said, adding that this was in spite of

Planes fit for snow, rain, heat and gloom of night

Throughout the 1920s, designers strove to produce planes that could carry the mail farther, faster and more economically—and in all kinds of weather as well. The aircraft shown here and on the following pages—with the dates they first flew noted next to their designations—were built to meet the demand for better carriers by the private airmail contractors that sprang up after 1925.

Following the formula set by the de Havilland D.H.4, most of the new designs were single-engined biplanes, with mail compartments set well forward and an open cockpit in the rear for improved visibility. One of the first was the Douglas M-2 *(below);* though only slightly faster than the D.H.4, it was easier to maintain and could carry 1,000 pounds of mail.

As light, air-cooled radial engines became widely available, designers began to provide smaller, more streamlined models such as the Pitcairn PA-5 and the Stearman C-3MB. Since these craft were economical to operate, they had particular appeal to small airlines whose profits depended primarily on carrying mail.

A couple of the planes also carried passengers. The Boeing 40—built specifically to fly mail over the high Western mountains—had room for two in its fully enclosed cabin. The last of the specialized mail craft, the advanced Northrop Alpha, could accommodate six passengers. Twelve of these all-metal monoplanes were purchased by TWA, which continued to fly them, despite their open cockpits, well into the 1930s.

DOUGLAS M-2 (1926)
Winner of a 1925 Post Office design competition, the M-2 used the same 400-hp Liberty engine that powered the D.H.4. This plane flew for Western Air Express.

BOEING 40B (1928)
A three-place combination cabin and open-cockpit biplane, the Boeing 40B was fitted with a 525-hp Pratt & Whitney Hornet radial engine. It flew for Boeing Air Transport, the forerunner of United Air Lines.

PITCAIRN PA-5 MAILWING (1928)
Powered by a 220-hp Wright Whirlwind engine, the tiny PA-5 had a wingspan of only 33 feet but could carry 500 pounds of mail 600 miles. This Pitcairn flew Eastern Air Transport's New York-Atlanta route.

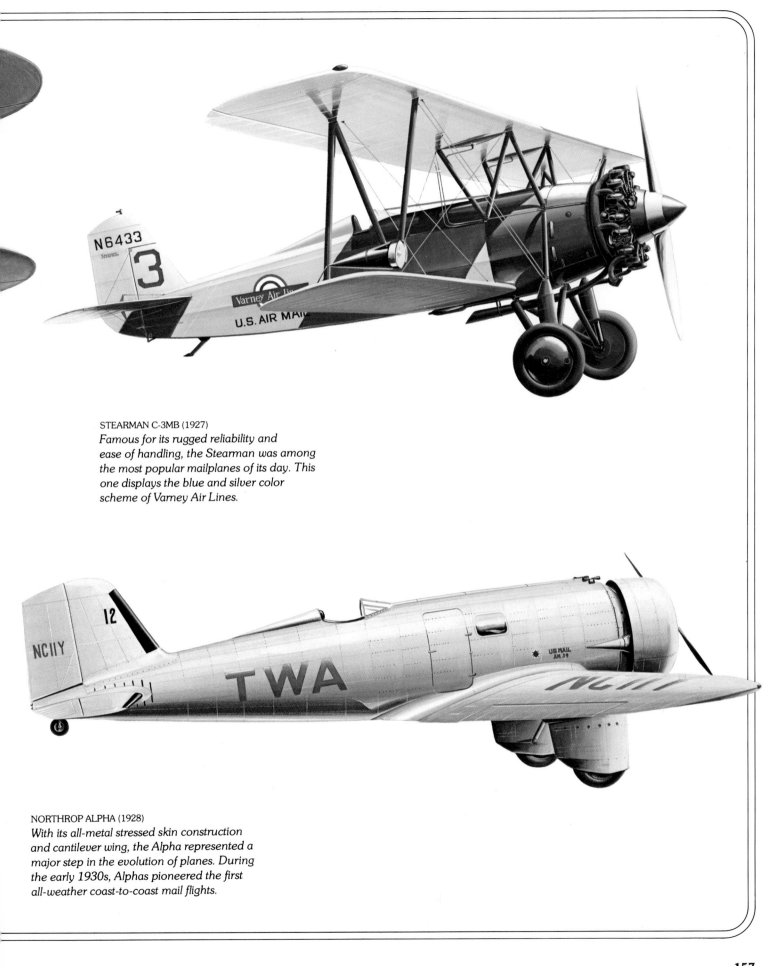

STEARMAN C-3MB (1927)
Famous for its rugged reliability and ease of handling, the Stearman was among the most popular mailplanes of its day. This one displays the blue and silver color scheme of Varney Air Lines.

NORTHROP ALPHA (1928)
With its all-metal stressed skin construction and cantilever wing, the Alpha represented a major step in the evolution of planes. During the early 1930s, Alphas pioneered the first all-weather coast-to-coast mail flights.

"sickening delays, night work putting planes together, and insufficiency of ships and motors unproved." One admirer of the Varney pilots presented Joe Taff with a timber-wolf pup. Taff kept the wolf in the hangar at Boise and took him along on flights when the mail load was light enough to permit a long-tailed passenger. The wolf loved to fly.

It was a little more than a year after Frank Rose's opening-day difficulties that Varney Air Lines suffered its first fatal accident. On April 15, 1927, pilot William E. Sanborn was en route to Boise from Salt Lake City—which had replaced remote Elko as the route's southern end in late 1926—when his Swallow ran into violent head winds in the Snake River valley at King Hill, Idaho. Witnesses said the plane was flying at about 200 feet when it abruptly climbed, turned and plunged to the ground. Sanborn was killed on impact. Shortly after Sanborn's death Varney began to replace the Swallows with more powerful Stearmans.

The first Stearman that Varney lost went down even before it was put into mail service. Factory pilot Frederick Hoyt was delivering one of the planes to Boise in January 1928 when he disappeared in a blizzard near Holbrook, Idaho. A week later the wreckage was sighted; Hoyt's body, wrapped in his parachute, was found 10 miles away. He had apparently bailed out and then died of exposure. In January 1929, pilot Harold Buckner was lost in similar whiteout conditions on a trip from Boise to Pasco. (By now, the Varney aviators were so well known that the headline in the Portland *Oregonian* read simply: "Harold Buckner Missing.") A pair of trappers found him immobilized and badly injured in his Stearman, which had smacked into a tree. The trappers improvised a litter and took the flier back to their cabin. One of the men then walked 15 miles through deep snow to report the news, but Buckner died of his injuries before a rescue party reached the cabin.

Such accidents had little effect on Varney's airmail customers or on his line's growing prosperity. Revenues were 40 per cent higher in 1928 than in 1927, while the performance record reached a respectable 90 per cent of flights attempted. The ambitious Varney was enjoying himself so much that he put in bids on five other contract routes, ranging as far east as Michigan and as far south as Mexico, but he was disappointed each time. Then in the summer of 1929 he secured his position in the Northwest by winning the route linking Portland, Seattle and Spokane with his Pasco-to-Salt Lake City service. Joe Taff flew the first Portland-to-Pasco trip on a mid-September evening when the smoke from forest fires was so thick that the recently installed beacons along the Columbia River gorge were invisible and all passenger planes were grounded.

By the following spring the Varney planes were flying passengers, too. Eventually the onetime nowhere line soon passed into the hands of the United Aircraft and Transport Corporation, the holding company that would become United Air Lines. Varney took in more than one million dollars from the sale of the line and tried several other aviation ventures before he eventually went broke. He surfaced later as a test pilot and finally as an operator of sand and gravel trucks.

The passing of the shirt-sleeve entrepreneurs like Varney, Dickinson and the Robertsons was symptomatic of the changes that were overtaking American aviation by the end of the 1920s. The mail lines, aided by generous government payload payments and by a cut in postage rates that boosted airmail usage by 95 per cent, were at last proving that aviation could be profitable. The airmail star was in the ascendant and nearly every major city was served by one or more air carriers: Route mileage had increased from 2,813 at the end of 1925 to 14,155 in 1928; the number of miles flown daily by mail pilots more than tripled between May 1928 and September 1929. The healthy profits, coupled with the development of better and larger planes, made passenger carrying an inevitable sequel, and by the end of 1929 almost all of the mail contractors were freighting human cargo along with their mail sacks. Aviation had become a big business that linked together most of the nation. The smaller regional operators were gradually swallowed up by corporate combines that eventually evolved into the major airlines such as Eastern, American, United and TWA.

By 1934 the days of the tempest-tossed lone aviator, bucking the odds daily to deliver the precious mail, seemed a nostalgic memory. The romance of man against nature had seemingly fled the American skies. Then, a Senate investigating committee charged that the Post Office had illegally favored large, influential airlines with lucrative mail routes. The head of the committee, Senator Hugo Black of Alabama, recommended that the federal government cancel all the airmail contracts. Postal officials asked Major General Benjamin Foulois, commander of the Army Air Corps, if his military fliers could step in and carry the mail in place of the airlines. Foulois replied that they could, and President Franklin D. Roosevelt issued the cancellation order on February 9, 1934; the Army would start flying the mail 10 days later.

Almost immediately, public figures began to speak out against the President's action. The humorist Will Rogers, writing two days after the airmail contracts were canceled, opined that the move was "like finding a crooked railroad president, then stopping all the trains." And Charles Lindbergh, the former airmail pilot who by now was a national idol, contended in a message to the President that the order "condemns the largest portion of our commercial aviation without just trial." The Air Corps's shaky preliminaries would only fuel the critical chorus.

Foulois and his deputies divided the route structure into three zones—Eastern, Central and Western—and decided not to stretch their meager peacetime resources too thin by trying to fly all of the 26 mail routes served by the commercial airlines. Instead, Army aviators would limit their operations to 14 routes that linked together the cities with Federal Reserve Banks; in that Depression year, it was essential to keep the nation's financial system functioning smoothly.

While Foulois was working out overall details, military mechanics hurriedly tried to adapt their various pursuit planes, bombers and observation craft for mail duty. The Air Corps was operating under severe

The government deals the domestic airlines a blow in this February 23, 1934, Washington Herald cartoon depicting the cancellation of airmail contracts with the lines. The government made this drastic move in response to charges of collusion and fraud in the awarding of the contracts.

handicaps. Funding for national defense had been trimmed considerably during the early 1930s, leaving the Army's air arm with a fleet of ill-equipped and largely obsolete planes. Few of the craft were fitted with instruments more sophisticated than those in the Post Office de Havillands of a decade earlier. Moreover, the military tactics of the time called for aircraft to be deployed almost exclusively during daylight hours, in relatively fair weather. As a consequence, most of the Army pilots had only the sketchiest acquaintance with either night flying or instrument flight, both of which were essential to get the mail through in midwinter.

Despite these shortcomings—and despite the fact that many military aviators would be piloting planes that they had not flown before—the officers in charge professed exuberant confidence in public. "We'll carry the mail, all right," said Major Byron Q. Jones, commander of the Eastern zone. "Don't worry about that unless an elephant drops on us, and if one does, we'll cut the elephant up and ship him out as air mail."

The elephant dropped on them three days before the Army's official debut as a mail carrier. On February 16, Lieutenants Jean D. Grenier and Edwin D. White were flying a Curtiss A-12 attack plane on a familiarization run over the jagged mountains between Cheyenne and Salt Lake City when they encountered snow and low clouds. Both officers were killed when their craft plowed into a mountainside not far from the place where civilian airmail pilot Hank Boonstra had barely survived a forced landing in similar conditions nearly 12 years earlier. Lieutenant James Y. Eastham, flying a Douglas Y1B-7 bomber over the old Varney route between Salt Lake City and Seattle, died that same day when he stalled while attempting to land in a snowstorm near Jerome, Idaho.

Now another prominent American added to the growing criticism of the government's new airmail policies. Edward V. Rickenbacker, the World War I fighter ace who had become an executive with Eastern Air Transport, one of the airlines that had lost its airmail contracts, reacted to news of the three deaths with a phrase that Roosevelt's political enemies would soon adopt: He called the fatalities "legalized murder."

Pressed into service during the 1934 mail crisis, a Thomas Morse O-19 reconnaissance plane (left), capable of carrying only 150 pounds of mail, soars above Oregon's Elkhorn Ridge. The heftier Curtiss A-12 attack plane (right) managed some 400 pounds loaded into its baggage compartment and gunner's cockpit.

Big enough to transport up to a ton of mail each, a pair of bombers—a Curtiss B-2 (left) and a Martin B-10—cruise over valleys in the rugged West. In the East, the newer, faster B-10 proved especially valuable on the heavy-volume New York-Chicago night runs and on the 1,200-mile route between Newark and Miami.

Most of the military aviators had time for only a few trial runs over routes that the commercial pilots had been flying day and night for years. On February 19, the first day the military airmen carried the mail, a severe storm howled across the East, dumping nine inches of snow in New York and 15 in New England. All planes were grounded, and trains were immobilized for two days; the few Army planes that got aloft that day were in the South and Midwest. There were no fatalities, but the flights were not without incident. Lieutenant Charles R. Springer, after trying three planes before he found one that would run, took off from St. Louis not long after 6 p.m. and headed for Indianapolis. Ten minutes later he was back: "Get me a flashlight," he said, "so I can find my way out of this damned town." His cockpit light had burned out, and he could not read his instruments or maps. Lieutenant John R. Sutherland, forced down by weather in Demopolis, Alabama, taxied his P-12 pursuit plane down the town's main street the next morning and filled his tank at an automobile service station before taking off again.

The Army's first week on the mail routes was an ordeal for everyone involved. Captain Ira C. Eaker, given command of the San Diego-Los Angeles-Salt Lake City route by Lieutenant Colonel Henry H. "Hap" Arnold, chief of the Western zone, was stunned to discover that the mail loads were much heavier than the Post Office had said they would be. "The stamp collectors were mainly responsible," Eaker recalled later. "The single-seat planes I had could carry about 50 pounds of mail, and the first day's load was 1,400 pounds." Arnold gave him permission to use a B-2 bomber, which could carry 2,000 pounds, but Eaker was the only pilot in his command who could fly a bomber. "I flew every trip that first week," he said. "I only took my clothes off to take a bath. My pilots had a week to learn how to fly a twin-engined bomber." Once they had managed that, Eaker stopped using lighter planes entirely. (Both Arnold and Eaker would gain renown in World War II, Arnold as head of the Army Air Forces and Eaker as commander of the Eighth Air Force.)

The weather throughout much of the country remained foul, and

161

with beacons now 10 to 15 miles apart on all mail routes, the Army pilots were told to come down at the nearest emergency field if they did not have beacon-to-beacon visibility and a ceiling of at least 500 feet. Then, on February 22, the Air Corps suffered its first fatality while actually carrying the mail: Lieutenant Durward O. Lowry crashed in dense fog while flying from Chicago to Cleveland. That evening, Lieutenant Harold L. Dietz drifted off course in fog and heavy rain over Maryland and circled the lights of a town three times while the fast-thinking residents tried to illuminate a field with their automobile headlights. Dietz clipped a tree and then struck a telephone pole in landing, suffering a fractured skull and internal injuries, but he survived.

Lieutenant George F. McDermott was not so lucky; the next day he drowned off the south shore of Long Island when the seaplane ferrying him and another pilot to Virginia developed engine trouble and had to land on the water. McDermott disappeared in the choppy sea before he could be rescued. Another pilot died in Texas that day when his plane hit a ditch and cartwheeled after being forced down by heavy rains.

In a raging blizzard, an Army Curtiss Falcon loaded with mail plows through snowdrifts on a Newark, New Jersey, runway, guided by an airport employee hanging onto the wing tip. Despite the weather that day, Army pilots flying out of Newark moved more than 4,000 pounds of mail.

The deaths of six pilots by the end of the Army's first official week of mail carrying switched the focus of the debate over the President's controversial decision from alleged contract irregularities to the Army Air Corps's own inadequacies. The predominantly anti-Roosevelt press loosed a volley of editorials blaming the fatalities on political machinations and calling for an immediate return to civilian mail flying. The country was "sick at heart," the *New York Herald Tribune* said. *The Los Angeles Times* observed that such slaughter was inevitable "when airplanes are put to uses for which they are not designed and pilots take up work in which they have no experience."

Brigadier General Oscar Westover, the officer in charge of the Army's airmail mission, blamed the misfortunes on the haste with which the men were sent into action. "When you consider how the job was dumped in our laps, and how little warning we had," he said, "the men have done exceptionally well, particularly with our present equipment."

These pilots were all killed in the early stages of Army airmail operations. Edwin White (top left) perished on a practice flight over Utah. Durward Lowry (top right) became the first Army flier killed on a scheduled mail run when he crashed in Ohio. Frederick Patrick (bottom left) went down in a storm in Texas while en route to Oklahoma to instruct Army mail pilots. George McDermott, forced down with engine trouble, drowned off Long Island.

Perhaps so, but it was a harrowing experience for many of them. Once, bomber pilot Beirne Lay was sent up in an unfamiliar pursuit plane on a frigid night over a route he did not know. The radio and compass failed as soon as he was aloft, and his railroad maps did not show beacons or emergency fields. He made it through, but the flight left him feeling like the Ancient Mariner. "I climbed out of the cockpit ahead of schedule," he reported, "but an old man, my eyes dim with the years."

After the first week of operations, General Foulois issued a strict set of safety orders. They prohibited planes without radios or navigational devices from flying at night, banned flights in icing conditions and held ground supervisors responsible for thorough inspections prior to takeoff. These new rules had the intended effect: There were a few minor mishaps and narrow escapes during the second week, but there were no deaths, and the clamorous opposition subsided somewhat. On the mail routes, there was even a light moment or two. One pilot took off resolutely into the night while his mail sacks still sat on the field; another flew a round trip and discovered at its end that he had delivered his mail back to its point of origin. But the most mortified pilot was undoubtedly the one who loaded his laundry bag in with his mail sacks and passed it along to the pilot flying the next leg. The laundry was later returned with a bill for $55 postage due.

Through it all, morale remained remarkably high, despite conditions that included danger, inadequate equipment and even a shortage of operating funds; red tape held up the money needed for living expenses and even tools. Curtis LeMay, a pilot on the Virginia-North Carolina run (he would later become the Air Force chief of staff), remembered that a mechanic who needed a particular wrench had to buy it at a local hardware store. The buoyant morale may have had something to do with a superabundance of what the young pilots liked best—flying time. "I haven't had so much fun since I've been in the Air Corps," one flier said. "There was so much hostility in the press, the accidents and dangers were magnified so," Ira Eaker recalled, "that we thought it would have a negative effect on morale. Instead it had the opposite effect: It made the pilots mad, and they tried that much harder."

The press may have magnified the dangers, but it did not invent them; the calamitous events of March 9, 1934, demonstrated that. The first Army airman to die that day was Private Ernest B. Sell, crewman on a mail-carrying bomber bound from Jacksonville to Miami. Sell's skull was crushed when he was thrown against the fuselage in a crash near Daytona Beach. Shortly after dark Lieutenant Otto Wienecke was killed when he crashed near Burton, Ohio, in heavy snow and near-zero visibility. Later that evening pilots Frank L. Howard and Arthur R. Kerwin were making a night familiarization flight out of Cheyenne. According to a newspaper account based on eyewitness reports, their engine began sputtering "like a Ford car operating on only two cylinders." As the fliers returned to the Cheyenne field their engine cut out completely, and the plane struck an electric

Launching the Britain-Central Africa route in the 1930s, an Armstrong-Whitworth Argosy draws Khartoum's curious.

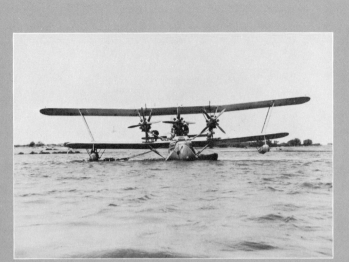

Anchored on the Nile in the 1930s, a Short Calcutta flying boat undergoes inspection. It could carry 15 passengers.

Boasting a 130-foot wingspan, a Handley Page H.P.42 receives the post from a mail van at London's Croydon field in 1935.

Passengers bound for Alexandria, Egypt, board a Short S.23 Empire flying boat for its maiden flight from Southampton in 1937.

The wings of empire

While the United States was developing airmail routes within its borders, Britain was extending its service to the Empire. It did so through a state-subsidized airline begun in 1923 with only 18 planes and 1,760 miles of European routes. Reorganized a year later, it was named Imperial Airways and soon had a fleet of three- and four-engined aircraft that could carry passengers as well as mail.

Connecting Britain and Basra, Iraq, via Cairo, on its first extended international run, Imperial eventually spread to India, Africa, the Far East and Australia. The volume of mail, however, remained low until 1938, when the government reduced the postal rate and loads doubled. But Imperial's days were numbered. In 1939, it was merged with the aggressive new British Airways into a single state-owned airline, BOAC—the British Overseas Airway Corporation.

SHORT-MAYO COMPOSITE
To span the North Atlantic, a Short S.20 seaplane named Mercury sits on top of a powerful S.21 flying boat called the Maia, forming the Short-Mayo composite, which used all eight engines for takeoff. When cruising altitude was reached, the Mercury separated from the Maia and went on its way. The Short-Mayo carried the mail for Imperial Airways on only two trial runs in 1938 before new developments in aviation rendered it obsolete.

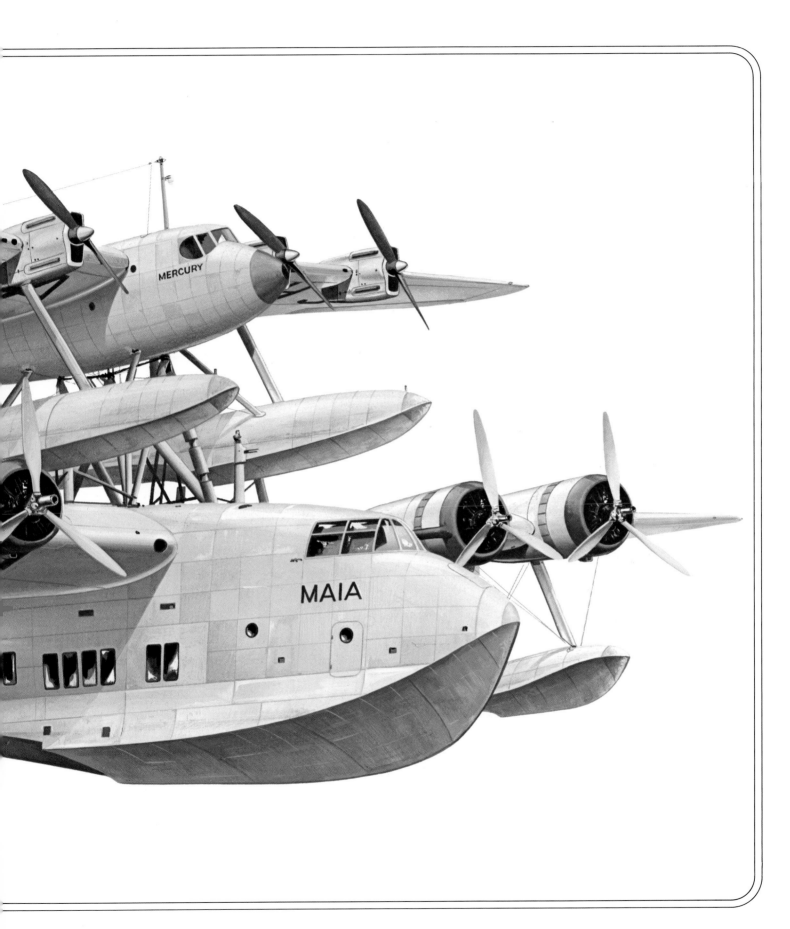

power line and caught fire. Both men perished in the burning wreck.

That single day's death toll brought the Army's total to 10 fatalities in just three weeks, and outrage swept the country. Bills had already been introduced in Congress to end the Army airmail flights and reopen the routes to the commercial airlines. President Roosevelt, under increasing pressure to act, summoned General Foulois and his superior, Army Chief of Staff General Douglas MacArthur, to the White House. "General," he demanded of Foulois, "when are these airmail killings going to stop?" Foulois answered: "Only when airplanes stop flying, Mr. President." This was followed by a 10-minute Presidential tirade that Foulois would recall as the worst tongue-lashing he ever received. Roosevelt issued a directive suspending mail flights except when routes and weather conditions would make fatal accidents nearly impossible. "The continuation of deaths in the Army Air Corps must stop," he declared. Foulois thereupon halted all airmail flights until the Army could regroup.

Military mechanics inspected and overhauled planes while the first shipments of the technically advanced Martin B-10 monoplane, an all-metal bomber, began to arrive. Foulois tightened the safety rules again, raising the minimum ceiling and requiring the mail fliers to have at least two years' service. The pilots practiced night and instrument flying. The number of routes was cut back from 14 to nine. Businessmen, meanwhile, improvised a stopgap airmail service by packaging their correspondence and sending it by express on commercial airlines.

On March 17, two days before the Army was due to resume its mail runs, pilot H. C. Richardson was killed on a training flight near Cheyenne. But Richardson's death turned out to be an exception to a general revival of the Army's competence and confidence. The stand-down proved beneficial: Improved equipment, better weather and the accumulation of experience all contributed to a greatly improved performance, and Army pilots began flying the mail as routinely as had their counterparts at the civilian airlines. Even so, the President and his postal officials realized that the Air Corps could not carry the mail indefinitely, and that the commercial air carriers needed mail revenues to help the nation maintain a healthy air transport system. The mail contracts were once more put up for bids from the airlines, and Army fliers made their final postal runs on May 7, 1934.

The end of the Army aviators' 78-day hitch as aerial postmen returned mail toting to its precrisis status as a job for passenger-carrying airliners. Once again it seemed that mail flying as a proud profession, a specialty with its own traditions and demands, had been overtaken by technology and rendered obsolete. And for the most part it had, until a Pennsylvania dentist devised a new way to exploit the old skills of the lone pilot and his single-engined plane flying the mail.

By the late 1930s, the nation was crisscrossed by airline routes, most of them plied by the large, twin-engined Douglas DC-3 that had revolutionized the air transport industry since its introduction in 1936. But there were many towns too small to warrant commercial air service; indeed, a number of these remote places did not even have airports. Dr. Lytle S. Adams, a dentist in the small southwestern Pennsylvania town of Irwin, did not believe that Irwin and other towns like it should thus be denied the benefits of direct airmail service. Adams had an answer: He invented a way for small planes to pick up and deliver sacks of mail without ever touching the ground.

Adams' method utilized a grappling hook lowered by a mechanic-mail clerk from a low-flying aircraft. The hook snatched a rope to which the outgoing mail sack was attached. The incoming sack was simply dropped from the plane. The company Adams formed in 1939, with the help of the wealthy Richard C. duPont of Delaware, was called All American Aviation and nicknamed "the airway to everywhere." Its area of operations, primarily in Pennsylvania and West Virginia, included the terrain that had made life adventurous for a generation of airmail pilots—the Hell Stretch of the Alleghenies.

The government authorized a one-year experimental operation of Adams' system beginning on May 12, 1939. All American's Stinson Reliant monoplanes, painted bright red and powered by 225-horsepower Lycoming engines, swooped over pickup stations in 54 towns on two routes out of Pittsburgh, one zigzagging east across Pennsylvania to Philadelphia and Wilmington, Delaware, and the other swinging south through the Ohio Valley and West Virginia. Some of the towns were not even on a railroad line; the smallest, Glenville, West Virginia, had a population of only 588.

The pickup stations, located from five to 20 miles apart, were established on high ground in pastures, schoolyards and cemeteries. A station consisted of two 30-foot-high steel poles set 60 feet apart, with a rope looped between them. The mailbag was attached to the rope, which was connected to the poles by spring clips that gave way when the four-fingered grappling hook engaged the rope as the pilot flew between the poles.

The pickup's opening day was less than a triumph. At Latrobe, Pennsylvania, the first attempt misfired when a stiff breeze blew the hook away from its target. The second try failed when a metal link holding the mailbag in place was broken. On the third effort the pilot dropped down to within about 20 feet of the rope, the hook made contact and the combination mail clerk-mechanic crouching in the Stinson's fuselage reeled the sack in as several hundred spectators shouted their approval.

The skill and precision demanded of aviators flying low over a notoriously spiny and often foggy landscape was so great that All American would not hire a pilot unless he had at least 10 years' experience and 4,000 hours in the air. But even these seasoned fliers had their harrowing moments as they flitted from hamlet to hamlet, seldom at altitudes above 500 feet. "I thought I was good, but I never realized what flying was until I started flying the pickup," All American pilot Junius "Toby" West Jr. would recall. "After a year I wanted to quit."

West stayed on, and like his fellow pickup pilots he learned to fly with his eyes focused on the land directly below. A particular landmark—a school, an oddly shaped rock, a grove of trees—was a signal to turn, to pull up, to drop the mail sack to the postal messenger waitng below. "If a farmer painted his barn a different color we'd be lost," said West.

All American's pilots faced hazards undreamed of by their open-cockpit predecessors on the early mail runs. Once, the retrieval equipment on a pickup plane was damaged when the grappling hook snagged a high-tension electric cable; on another occasion, a hook hit the ground and then bounced wildly back into the air, spinning the retrieval line around the plane's wing. The pilot set down in a nearby field, unwrapped the line and flew on to complete his mail run.

The pickup planes proved to be far more versatile than more conventional means of transport. When the Ohio River valley was flooded in April 1940, halting buses and trains and grounding the airlines, All American's planes continued to fly on schedule; rowboats ferried the mail sacks to the air pickup stations.

Following the success of All American's trial year of operations, the Civil Aeronautics Board certified the line as the only air carrier dedicated solely to flying mail and express. Soon, All American was improving its equipment—planes were fitted with a retractable boom to help guide the dangling retrieval rope—and adding new routes to its system. By the summer of 1941 the line was serving more than 100 cities and towns and picking up some 400,000 pieces of mail per month.

All American tried repeatedly to gain Civil Aeronautics Board approval to extend the airmail pickup to other regions of the country. But the board—which supervised the federal postal payments to the airlines—had begun to lean away from relatively expensive pickup operations, favoring instead the establishment of more economical feeder airlines that would fly paying passengers as well as mail on routes not served by the major carriers. All American dropped its pickup operations in 1949 and converted to passenger carrying. Two years later, the line changed its name to Allegheny Airlines; later still, it would become USAir.

Toby West and many of his fellow pickup pilots adjusted easily to the inevitable change and stayed on, switching from rugged Stinsons to 24-seat DC-3s that carried passengers along with the mail. For them, as for earlier generations of mail pilots who had pioneered the world's airways for the great commercial airlines, an era in the history of aviation had ended. But, like the veterans of the old United States Air Mail Service, the French Aéropostale and the contract mail lines of the late 1920s, like the ocean-straddling, jungle-hopping Lufthansa aviators of the 1930s, they would cherish the memory of their years of flying the mail. No amount of change or progress could deprive them of that. And West, who had been among the last of that venturesome breed, might have been speaking for mail pilots throughout the world when he mused long afterward: "We were free and independent, and we flew the way we wanted to. I loved it. I wish it had never stopped." ﹏

Swooping over a Pennsylvania hill, a Fairchild monoplane

reels in a mailbag in a 1930 trial. By trailing a cable through the slotted V-shaped structure on the left, the plane could snag a sack left hanging there.

Acknowledgments

The index for this book was prepared by Gale Linck Partoyan. For their valuable help in the preparation of this volume, the editors wish to thank: **In France:** Nancy—Charles Laprévote; Nice—Marceau Méresse; Orly—Jean Lasserre, *Icare;* Paris—Gérard Baschet, Éditions de l'*Illustration;* Jean Macaigne; André Bénard, Odile Benoist, Elisabeth Bonhomme, Alain Degardin, Georges Delaleau, Gilbert Deloizy, Yvan Kayser, Général Pierre Lissarague, Director, Jean-Yves Lorent, Stéphane Nicolaou, Général Roger de Ruffray, Deputy Director, Pierre Willefert, Curator, Musée de l'Air; Edmond Petit, Curator, Musée Air-France; Hélène de Vogüe; Rambouillet—Victor Beaufol. **In Great Britain:** London—Miss E. A. Flint, Bruce Castle Museum; Colonel R. N. R. P. James, Commandant, British Forces Post Office; Peter Johnson, Phillips Auctioneers; Elizabeth Moore, *Illustrated London News;* Arnold Nayler, Royal Aeronautical Society; Tony Gammons, P. G. Howe, R. W. Jones, Post Office; Anthony C. Harold, David I. Roberts, RAF Museum;

Martin Andrewartha, John Bagley, Science Museum; R. F. S. West, Philatelic Collection, British Library; Sutton Coldfield—Francis J. Field. **In Italy:** Rome—Fiorenza De Bernardi; Contessa Maria Fede Caproni, Museo Aeronautico Caproni di Taliedo; Museo delle Poste e delle Telecomunicazioni. **In Japan:** Tokyo—Tadashi Nozawa; Communications Museum of the Ministry of Post and Telecommunications. **In the United States:** California—Edwin O. Cooper; Dr. James Duffy; Harlan Gurney; Emil Henrich; Jerome F. Lederer; E. Hamilton Lee; Bruce Reynolds, San Diego Aerospace Museum; Dean C. Smith; R. L. Wagner; Washington, D.C.—Jerry Clark, National Archives and Records Service; R. E. G. Davies, Philip Edwards, Paul Garber, Pete Suthard, National Air and Space Museum; General Ira Eaker; Reidar Norby, National Philatelic Collection, National Museum of American History; Florida—Charles F. Devoe; John R. Hadley; Paula Musto, Eastern Airlines; Illinois—Chuck Novak, United Airlines; Maryland—Dr. Richard P. Hallion Jr., University

of Maryland; New York—Carl Apollonio, Crown Publishers; H. F. Bradybaugh; Wayne Hilleson; Merrill Stickler, Glenn H. Curtiss Museum; Pennsylvania—Charles E. Gates; Daniel W. Hines; Jim Kerschner; Utah—Henry Boonstra; Roy Gibson; Virginia—Louis S. Casey; Junius M. West; Wyoming—Emmett D. Chisum, Paula McDougall, American Heritage Center, University of Wyoming. **In West Germany:** Cologne—Werner Bittner, Deutsche Lufthansa; West Berlin—Heidi Klein, Dr. Roland Klemig, Bildarchiv Preussischer Kulturbesitz; Eva Bong, Wolfgang Streubel, Ullstein Bilderdienst.

Particularly useful sources of information and quotations used in this volume were: *Air Mail Emergency, 1934* by Norman Borden, The Bond Wheelwright Company, 1968; *The Airmail: Jennies to Jets* by Benjamin Lipsner, Wilcox and Follett Company, 1951; "Six Million Miles: The Story of Varney Airlines" by Barrett Tillman, *American Aviation Historical Society Journal,* Fall 1971, Winter 1971 (2 parts).

Bibliography

Books

Borden, Norman E., Jr., *Air Mail Emergency, 1934.* The Bond Wheelwright Company, 1968.

Bowers, Peter M., *Yesterday's Wings.* Aircraft Owners and Pilots Association, 1974.

Cate, Curtis, *Antoine de Saint-Exupéry.* Putnam, 1970.

Culver, Edith Dodd, *The Day the Air-Mail Began.* Cub Flyers Enterprises, Inc., no date.

Daurat, Didier, *Dans le vent des hélices.* Paris: Éditions du Seuil, 1956.

David, Paul T., *The Economics of Air Mail Transportation.* The Brookings Institution, 1934.

Davies R. E. G., *A History of the World's Airlines.* London: Oxford University Press, 1964.

Field, Francis J., and N. C. Baldwin, *The Coronation Aerial Post, 1911.* Sutton Coldfield, England: Francis J. Field, Ltd., 1934.

Fleury, J. G., *L'Atlantique sud de l'Aéropostale à Concorde.* Paris: Denoël, 1974.

Foulois, Benjamin D., and Carroll V. Glines, *From the Wright Brothers to the Astronauts.* Arno Press, 1980.

Goldstrom, John, *A Narrative History of Aviation.* Macmillan, 1980.

Harper, Harry, and Robert Brenard, *The Romance of the Flying Mail.* London: George Routledge & Sons, Ltd., 1933.

Higham, Robin, *Britain's Imperial Air Routes, 1918 to 1939: The Story of Britain's Overseas Airlines.* The Shoe String Press, 1961.

Hill, Roderic, *The Baghdad Air Mail.* Longmans, Green & Co., 1929.

Hopkins, George E., *The Airline Pilots: A Study in Elite Unionization.* Harvard University Press, 1971.

Juptner, Joseph P., *U.S. Civil Aircraft,* Vol. 1. Aero, 1962.

Komons, Nick A., *Bonfires to Beacons.* Federal Aviation Administration, 1978.

Kronstein, Dr. Max, *Pioneer Airpost Flights of the World, 1830-1935.* American Air Mail Society, 1978.

Lipsner, Benjamin B., *The Airmail: Jennies to Jets.* Wilcox and Follett Company, 1951.

Lufthansa Story, The. Cologne: Lufthansa German Airlines, 1980.

Mackay, James Alexander, *Airmails, 1870-1970.* London: B. T. Batsford Ltd., 1971.

Mayborn, Mitch, and Peter M. Bowers, *Stearman Guidebook.* Flying Enterprise Publications, 1972.

Migeo, Marcel, *Saint-Exupéry.* London: Macdonald, 1961.

Moore, Byron, *The First Five Million Miles.* Arno Press, 1980.

O'Sullivan, Thomas J., and Karl B. Weber, *History of the United States Pioneer and Government-Operated Air Mail Service, 1910-1928.* American Air Mail Society, 1973.

Petee, Frank, *The Triple A Story, 1938-1946.* Allegheny Airlines, 1964.

Ross, Walter S., *The Last Hero: Charles A. Lindbergh.* Harper & Row, 1976.

Rumbold, Richard, and Lady Margaret Stewart, *The Winged Life: A Portrait of Antoine de Saint-Exupéry, Poet and Airman.* David M. McKay, 1953.

Scamehorn, Howard L., *Balloons to Jets.* Henry Regnery Company, 1957.

Schamburger, Page, *Tracks Across The Sky: The Story of the Pioneers of the U.S. Air Mail.* Lippincott, 1964.

Schlesinger, Arthur M., Jr., *The Age of Roosevelt: The Coming of the New Deal.* Houghton Mifflin, 1958.

Smith, Dean C., *By the Seat Of My Pants.* Little,

Brown, 1961.

Smith, Henry Ladd, *Airways: A History of Commercial Aviation in the United States.* Alfred A. Knopf, 1942.

Stroud, John, *European Transport Aircraft Since 1910.* London: Putnam, 1966.

Taylor, Frank J., *High Horizons: Daredevil Flying Postmen to Modern Magic Carpet—The United Air Lines Story.* McGraw-Hill, 1951.

Warner, Edward Pearson, *The Early History of Air Transportation.* Norwich University, 1938.

Whitehouse, Arch, *The Sky's The Limit: A History of the U.S. Airlines.* Macmillan, 1971.

Periodicals

Bell, Luther K., "The Future of the Air Mail." *The Outlook,* January 28, 1923.

Downs, Eldon W., "Army and the Airmail—1934." *The Airpower Historian,* January 1962.

Ham, Géo, "Comment, en Huit Jours, Un Sac de Courrier est acheminé de Paris à Santiago." *L'Illustration,* November 19, 1932.

Lindbergh, Charles A., "Mailman Overboard!" *Popular Aviation,* May 1938.

Patterson, Richard, "The Army flies the U.S. Air Mail." *Aviation Quarterly,* Vol. 2, No. 4, no date.

Silver, Philip, "Someone Wrote to the President." *The American Philatelist,* April 1978.

Tillman, Barrett, "Six Million Miles: The Story of Varney Air Lines." *American Aviation Historical Society Journal,* Fall 1971, Winter 1971.

Van Zandt, J. Parker, "On the Trial of the Air Mail." *The National Geographic Magazine,* January 1926.

Woodhouse, Henry, "The Inauguration of the New York-Philadelphia-Washington Aerial Mail Line." *Flying,* June 1918.

Picture credits

The sources for the illustrations that appear in this book are listed below. Credits for the illustrations from left to right are separated by semicolons; from top to bottom they are separated by dashes.

Endpaper (and cover detail, regular edition): Painting by Paul Lengellé. 7: Henry Beville, courtesy Collection of E. Hamilton Lee. 8: The Bettmann Archive. 9, 10: UPI. 11: Smithsonian Institution (No. 75-7024). 12: UPI. 13: Alaska Historical Library. 14, 15: Jesse Davidson Air Mail History Archives. 16, 17: The Bettmann Archive. 18: By permission of the British Library. 19: Musée Air-France, Paris—Aldo Durazzi, courtesy Museo Aeronautico Caproni di Taliedo, Rome. 20: The Bettmann Archive. 21: Jesse Davidson Air Mail History Archives. 22: Musée de l'Air, Paris—courtesy of the British Post Office. 23: Lufthansa, Cologne—Musée de l'Air, Paris—Lufthansa, Cologne. 26: Smithsonian Institution (No. 78-7216). 29: Jesse Davidson Air Mail History Archives. 31: The Bettmann Archive. 32: Courtesy United Airlines. 33: Daniel W. Hines. 34, 35: Drawing by John Batchelor. 37-39: Jesse Davidson Air Mail History Archives. 40, 41: Leon Dishman, courtesy National Air and Space Museum, Smithsonian Institution. 42, 43: Courtesy United Airlines, insets, Smithsonian Institution (No. 47828-G); Jesse Davidson Air Mail History Ar-

chives. 44, 45: Culver Pictures, inset, Jesse Davidson Air Mail History Archives. 46, 47: Jesse Davidson Air Mail History Archives, except center inset, The Bettmann Archive. 48, 49: Jesse Davidson Air Mail History Archives. 50, 51: Library of Congress. 53-69: Jesse Davidson Air Mail History Archives. 70, 71: Charles F. Devoe Collection, background, © *Model Airplane News* Magazine, from *The Best of Wylam,* published by Air Age, Inc., 1979, Darien, Connecticut. 72, 73: Jesse Davidson Air Mail History Archives, background, © *Model Airplane News* Magazine, from *The Best of Wylam,* published by Air Age, Inc., 1979, Darien, Connecticut. 74, 75: Charles F. Devoe Collection, background, © *Model Airplane News* Magazine, published by Air Age, Inc., 1979, Darien, Connecticut. 76-81: Jesse Davidson Air Mail History Archives. 82, 83: Drawing by John Batchelor. 85-89: Jesse Davidson Air Mail History Archives. 90: National Archives. 91: National Archives (No. 28-MS-1D-1); Jesse Davidson Air Mail History Archives—National Archives; Jesse Davidson Air Mail History Archives. 92, 93: Jesse Davidson Air Mail History Archives. 95: Leon Dishman, courtesy National Air and Space Museum, Smithsonian Institution. 97, 99: Jesse Davidson Air Mail History Archives. 100-103: National Philatelic Collection, Smithsonian Institution. 104: Phillips, International Fine Arts Auction-

eers, London—Collection of Communications Museum of the Ministry of Post and Telecommunications, Tokyo; by permission of the British Library. 105: Courtesy of the British Post Office—Henry Beville, courtesy National Philatelic Collection, Smithsonian Institution—Aldo Durazzi, courtesy Museo Aeronautico Caproni di Taliedo, Rome; Henry Beville, courtesy National Philatelic Collection, Smithsonian Institution (2). 106, 107: Musée Air-France, Paris. 109: Technisches Museum, Vienna. 110: Musée Air-France, Paris. 114, 115: *Revue Icare,* Paris. 116: Musée Air-France, Paris. 117: Courtesy Musée de l'Air, Paris. 118-121: Musée Air-France, Paris. 123-126: Courtesy l'*Illustration,* France. 128, 129: Dmitri Kessel, courtesy Musée de l'Air, Paris. 130, 131: Drawings by John Batchelor. 132: Musée Air-France, Paris. 133-135: Collection Jean Macaigne, Paris. 136-145: Lufthansa, Cologne. 146: Courtesy of the Illinois State Historical Library. 150-153: Jesse Davidson Air Mail History Archives. 155-157: Drawings by John Batchelor. 159: © 1934, Winsor Macay for the Washington, D.C., *Herald,* courtesy the Library of Congress. 160-162: Jesse Davidson Air Mail History Archives. 163: UPI. 165: Courtesy Collection of Ron Davies (2)—courtesy of the British Post Office; BBC Hulton Picture Library, London. 166, 167: Drawing by John Batchelor. 170, 171: UPI.

Index